Simon and Alison Holst

Kiwi Favourites

New Zealand's most popular recipes

David Bateman

Text © Simon and Alison Holst, 2008
Typographical design © David Bateman Ltd, 2008

First published in 2008 by David Bateman Ltd,
30 Tarndale Grove, Albany, Auckland, New Zealand

Reprinted in 2009

ISBN 978-1-86953-722-7

Designed and typeset by Grace Design
Photographs by Lindsay Keats
Kiwi chef symbol by Errol McLeary
Printed in China through Colorcraft Ltd, Hong Kong

Contents

Weights & Measures

The following measures have been used in this book:

1 teaspoon (tsp)	5ml
1 tablespoon (Tbsp)	15ml
¼ cup	60ml
½ cup	125ml
1 cup	250ml
4 cups	1litre

All the cup and spoon measures are level, unless otherwise stated. (Rounded or heaped measures will upset the balance of ingredients.) Flour is measured spooned (rather than scooped or packed) into measuring cups. Most butter quantities are given by weight, however small amounts are measured by tablespoon. One tablespoon weighs 15g.

If you are weighing in ounces and pounds, use the following approximations:

30g	1oz
60g	2oz
90g	3oz
105g	3.5oz
120g	4oz
150g	5oz
180g	6oz
220g	7oz
250g	8oz
500g	1lb
1kg	2lb

If you are measuring in inches, use the following approximations:

5mm	¼in
1cm	½in
2.5cm	1in
10cm	4in
12cm	5in
15cm	6in
18cm	7in
20cm	8in
23cm	9in
25cm	10in
30cm	12in

Abbreviations:

mm	millimetre
cm	centimetre
in	inch
C	Celsius
F	Fahrenheit
ml	millilitre
l	litre
g	gram
kg	kilogram
oz	ounce
lb	pound

Temperatures and approximate equivalents:

Celsius	Fahrenheit	Gas
150°C	300°F	2
160°C	325°F	3
170°C	325°F	3
180°C	350°F	4
190°C	375°F	5
200°C	400°F	6
210°C	425°F	7
220°C	425°F	7
230°C	450°F	8
250°C	500°F	9

Always bring the oven to the required temperature before putting in the food which is to be cooked, unless specified. If you use an oven which does not have a fan, you may find that you need to allow a slightly longer cooking time, or a slightly higher temperature.

Can sizes:
Can sizes may vary; do not worry if the cans are a little larger or smaller than those specified. Small differences are unlikely to affect your recipe.

Cooking times:
Because ovens and microwave ovens vary so much, you should take the cooking times suggested in these recipes as a guide only. The first time you make a recipe, check at intervals to make sure it is not cooking faster, or more slowly, than expected.

Always follow the detailed instructions given by the manufacturers of your appliances and equipment rather than the more general instructions given in these recipes.

Introducing Kiwi Favourites

Although we would have been happy to fill this book with our own favourite recipes, this is not what we felt we should do.

Our extended families, when questioned, responded enthusiastically with the names of many of their favourite foods. Next we approached friends, who widened our range of recipes considerably. Excited by this response, we kept asking questions. We asked eight-year-olds to 80-year-olds. We handed out questionnaires to groups of men and women at a wide variety of work places, and to members of different recreational groups. (Many thanks to all the Kiwis who were so interested in our project and were so helpful.)

Eventually, when we felt that we had gone about as far as we could, we took our piles of papers to the computer. We found it very exciting to see the results. We had expected to see some of them, but not others! This book contains the recipes with the largest numbers of votes. The recipes which were the most popular appear first in each section and are accompanied by the little kiwi chef symbol you can see below.

We asked for just recipe names, so our next job was to write the recipes themselves. We have tried to keep these fairly simple, but hope we have given enough details to help cooks who are trying something quite different for the first time.

We also hope our book will be of interest to visitors to our beautiful country. We would like to help them remember some of the foods they ate while touring, so once home again, they can prepare the same things in their own kitchens.

Wherever you come from, and wherever you may be, we hope that you will enjoy preparing and eating the dishes which truly are Kiwi favourites.

Simon & Alison Holst

The little kiwi chef symbol tells you which recipe was the favourite in each section.

Soups & Starters

GOOD OLD PUMPKIN SOUP TOPPED OUR SOUP POLL, BUT DELICIOUS MUSSEL CHOWDER WAS CLOSE BEHIND, AND IS CERTAINLY WORTH TRYING! AND THESE POPULAR STARTERS, TASTY AND EASY TO MAKE, ARE GREAT AS DIPS OR SPREAD ON CRUSTY BREAD.

PUMPKIN SOUP

Pumpkin Soup

There is something particularly soothing about a bowl of smooth and creamy pumpkin soup on a cold winter's day. This recipe suggests several alternatives, so you can ring the changes, varying the flavour of your soup as it suits you. In early autumn, you might find that you have a thinner mixture, as the earlier pumpkins don't tend to be as floury as those which mature some months later.

For 4–6 servings

2 Tbsp canola oil or butter
1 large onion
2 cloves garlic, optional
500–600g prepared pumpkin
1 tsp curry powder
1 tsp ground cumin, optional
4 cups vegetable or chicken stock
    or 4 cups water plus 3 tsp instant
    chicken or vegetable stock
extra liquid if purée is too thick
about 1 cup of milk or canned
    coconut cream, optional

- Put the oil or butter in a fairly large pot which has a lid. Chop the halved and peeled onion into small cubes, chop the garlic finely, and add to the pan. Cover and cook over low heat, stirring often, until the onion is transparent but not browned.
- Meanwhile, chop the pumpkin into manageable pieces and remove and discard the skin and seeds. Cut the pumpkin into 2–3cm chunks. (You usually need about 1kg pumpkin, as bought, for 500–600g prepared pumpkin.)
- Before adding the pumpkin to the pot, stir the curry powder (and cumin) into the transparent onion mixture until the spices smell fragrant. Add the prepared pumpkin, then the stock of your choice, bring to the boil then cover and simmer until the pumpkin is tender, probably about 20 minutes.
- Purée the mixture, adding extra water, stock, milk or coconut cream if purée is too thick. Adjust seasonings to taste, adding a little salt, sugar and pepper as desired.
- Refrigerate if necessary and reheat when required.

French Onion Soup

Whenever we make this classic soup, we wonder why we don't make it more often. It is quick and simple, especially if you have a food processor, and really versatile. It makes a good starter for a formal meal or, if you add the cheesy croutons, it can be the basis of a more casual meal.

For 4–6 servings

1kg (about 5 medium) onions
2 Tbsp olive or canola oil
2 Tbsp balsamic vinegar
½–1 tsp dried thyme
4 cups vegetable or chicken stock
½–1 cup dry white wine
about 1 tsp salt
pepper to taste

- Halve, peel and thinly slice the onions (a food processor fitted with the slicing blade does this very efficiently). Heat the oil in a large, heavy pot then add the onions. Cook, stirring frequently until the onions have softened and are beginning to brown (about 10–15 minutes), then add the balsamic vinegar and the thyme. Continue to cook, stirring frequently and watching closely so the onion doesn't catch on the bottom and burn. Cook until the mixture is well browned (this browning gives the soup much of its final colour and flavour).
- Stir in the stock and wine and season to taste. Bring the mixture to the boil, then reduce the heat and simmer gently for a further 15–20 minutes.
- Check the seasonings again, then serve. Add Cheesy Croutons (below) and a green salad on the side to make a really easy meal.

Cheesy Croutons

The traditional way to prepare these is to ladle the soup into individual bowls, cover the top of each bowl with sliced bread and sprinkle generously with grated cheese. The bowls are then placed under the grill until the cheese is golden brown.

- To avoid having to get hot, soup-filled bowls in and out of the oven, we prefer to cheat and make the croutons separately. Simply arrange slices of bread on a baking sheet, grill the first side until golden, then turn them over, sprinkle with grated cheese, and grill again until golden brown. These croutons can then be floated on top of the individual bowls or served alongside the soup.

Smoked Salmon Dip or Spread

This delicious dip has the attractive colour and appealing flavour of hot-smoked salmon. It can be used as a popular spread, too.

For about 1½ cups

100–150g hot or cold smoked salmon
250g carton cream cheese
2 Tbsp lemon juice
1–2 Tbsp capers
1–2 Tbsp horseradish cream (optional)
about 2 Tbsp chopped parsley, dill or
    chives (optional)
salt and pepper to taste

- Put the salmon, cream cheese and lemon juice into a food processor and process until well mixed but not completely smooth. Add the capers, horseradish (if using) and the chopped herbs of your choice, and process again, just enough to mix.
- Season to taste then cover and refrigerate until required. (Although it tastes good when eaten straight away, its flavour is even better after a couple of hours.)
- Serve spread on crusty bread, crackers, etc, as a dip for vegetable crudités, or with lettuce or cucumber as an easy sandwich/roll filling.

Creamy Mussel Chowder

Cultivated live mussels, widely available in supermarkets, make wonderful chowder, which tastes even better than the soups you may have made with mussels gathered from rocks at the beach. These days, unless you're really confident about the water quality, it's probably safer to use farmed mussels in chowder.

For 3–4 servings

1kg live cultivated mussels in shells
1 large or 2 medium onions
1 Tbsp canola or other oil
1 large carrot
2 large celery stalks
2 medium-sized potatoes
50g butter
½ cup plain flour
2 cups milk
2 cups reserved cooking liquid
salt and pepper to taste
chopped fresh parsley or dill

- Boil 2 cups of water in a large pot, add a third of the washed mussels, cover and heat until the shells open, then lift them immediately into a large bowl. Repeat until all mussels have opened; discard those which haven't opened. Save the liquid.
- Cut the onions into 1cm cubes, then cook without browning in the oil, in a fairly large, non-stick, covered pan, stirring occasionally. Cut the carrots, celery and potatoes into similar cubes, and add to the pan, with the strained liquid from the pot. Cover and simmer until all the vegetables are tender. Drain and reserve the liquid.
- Remove mussels from shells and cut into 1cm chunks, discarding any beards, etc. Refrigerate the chopped mussels and add any liquid from them to the pan.
- Melt the butter in the cleaned mussel pot, then stir in the flour. Add the milk and bring to the boil, stirring or whisking constantly, then add the liquid from the cooked vegetables, bring to the boil again and turn off the heat.
- Add the hot cooked vegetables to the pot and season the mixture carefully to taste. If not serving immediately, cool and refrigerate up to 24 hours.
- When ready to serve, heat the mixture in the pot over moderate heat, until very hot, stirring constantly, making sure nothing burns on the bottom. When heated through, add two-thirds of the chopped mussels and any liquid from them, then pour the chowder into large bowls. Top with the remaining mussels, add the chopped parsley or dill and serve with hot rolls, garlic bread or toast. Let diners add crème fraiche, sour cream, or yoghurt if they wish.

SMOKED SALMON DIP OR SPREAD

Hasty Hummus

Good old hummus is a delicious and versatile food. Served with vegetable crudités and wedges of pita bread it makes a delicious snack or light meal, but it is also delicious used as a spread in sandwiches and rolls. (It sounds plain, but wheatmeal bread, hummus and sliced olives make a delicious sandwich.)

'Plain' hummus is just fine, but when you feel like something a little different, try the Pumpkin & Peanut version given below.

For 1½ cups

1 large clove garlic
300–400g can chickpeas (see note
  below)
2 Tbsp tahini (see note below)
2 Tbsp lemon juice
2–3 Tbsp olive oil
¼ tsp salt
water or chickpea liquid to thin
  (if required)

- Process the garlic and drained chickpeas with the metal chopping blade, until finely chopped. Add the tahini and lemon juice. When evenly mixed add 2 Tbsp of the oil and salt. Process until very smooth, stopping once or twice to scrape down the sides, adding the extra oil, water or chickpea liquid to thin to the desired consistency. Taste and add a little extra salt if needed.
- Serve immediately with vegetable crudités and/or warmed pita wedges, or transfer to an airtight container and store in the fridge for 3–5 days.

NOTE:

- *Simon likes to drain and rinse the chickpeas, but Alison drains them, reserves the liquid and uses it to thin the hummus if required – you can do whichever you prefer!*
- *Tahini is a paste made from ground sesame seeds. It's available in larger supermarkets and is often found with the pre-prepared dips and spreads or Middle Eastern foods.*

Pumpkin & Peanut Hummus

- Place 100g peeled and cubed pumpkin in a small microwave bowl, cover and microwave on high (100%) for two minutes. Add the cooked pumpkin to the processor with the chickpeas and garlic. Replace the tahini with 2 Tbsp peanut butter and for a slight twist, add ¼ tsp curry powder as well, then proceed as above.

Easy Guacamole

Guacamole makes a great 'ready-in-a-minute' dip for corn chips or crudités — and a dollop will improve almost any snack. Grab a ready-to-use avocado (its flesh will 'give' slightly at this stage) whenever you see a nice one in the supermarket.

For about 1 cup

1 ripe avocado
2 Tbsp lemon juice
1 finely chopped spring onion
¼ tsp salt
Tabasco sauce to taste
chopped coriander leaves, optional

- Cut around the centre of the avocado lengthways, then gently twist the two halves apart. Chop a sharp knife into the stone and twist it to remove the stone.
- Spoon the flesh into a bowl, scraping out the greenest flesh close to the shell. Mash with a fork, and add the remaining ingredients, using quantities to suit your taste. Use immediately or cover with cling film touching the surface and leave for no longer than an hour before using.
- Use as a dip for corn chips, as a topping for Mexican foods, crackers, crostini, and in other ways you like.

Lunches &
Light Meals

WE LOVE THE VARIETY OF THE RECIPES IN THIS SECTION. FOREIGN FAVOURITES
AND EGG DISHES WE HAVE BEEN BROUGHT UP WITH AND STILL LOVE —
WHAT A GREAT MIXTURE!

EGGS BENEDICT

Eggs Benedict

We tend to use the name 'Eggs Benedict' rather loosely! When we serve poached eggs on toasted English muffins topped with Hollandaise Sauce, we call them this. What makes us feel a bit guilty is that between the poached egg and the toasted English muffin we sometimes put ham, but at other times we put smoked salmon or well-drained, freshly cooked spinach. All are delicious, but we should call each a different name. You can call them whatever you like!

For 2 servings

Hollandaise Sauce
the yolk of 1 large egg
2 tsp lemon juice
50g butter

1 split English muffin
several slices of thinly sliced ham or
    several slices of smoked salmon or
    about 12 spinach leaves, cooked
    and well drained
2 large eggs, poached

- First make the Hollandaise Sauce. Break the egg yolk into a food processor or a smaller similar machine, and add the lemon juice. Cut the butter into cubes and place in a covered Pyrex measuring cup or something similar. Loosely cover the top and microwave it on High for 60–90 seconds, until it is very hot and bubbling vigorously.
- Turn the food processor on and add the very hot butter to the egg yolk in a steady stream until the mixture thickens. (You can make this ahead and re-warm it by standing it in a container of bath-temperature water if you like.)
- Toast the halved muffin, get the ham or salmon ready, or cook and drain the spinach. Warm the plates you are going to use.
- Poach the eggs in simmering water containing ½ tsp of salt and 1 Tbsp of white wine vinegar. After 2–3 minutes, or when they are as firm as you like, lift the eggs carefully onto the toasted, topped, muffin halves, spoon the warm Hollandaise Sauce over them, and serve immediately.

French Omelet

A French Omelet makes an quick but interesting breakfast or lunch. We were pleased to see that many Kiwis listed an omelet as one of their favourite foods! It takes only a few minutes to make, requires the minimum amount of mess, time and money, and can have all sorts of fillings (including leftovers) hidden inside it.

For 1 serving
1 large egg
1 Tbsp milk
pinch of salt
pepper to taste
2 tsp butter

- Use a non-stick pan or a pan with a good, smooth finish, about 18–20cm from edge to edge, for a one-egg omelet. (If you only have a bigger pan, make a two-egg omelet, doubling all the ingredients.) Make sure the pan is very smooth, clean and dry. Rub a non-stick pan with a little oil if necessary, or rub a pan without a similar finish with dry salt on a paper towel to make the surface smooth, then oil it lightly.
- Measure the first four ingredients into a small bowl and beat with a fork until well mixed but not frothy.
- Put the pan over moderate heat. When you can hold your hand above it and feel that it is warm, add the butter quickly and swirl it round the pan. It should bubble but not burn. Before it browns, tip in all the egg mixture and have a stirrer or flexible spatula ready to lift the edge of the omelet in two or three places, so that the liquid on top can run underneath.
- As soon as there is no runny egg mixture left, flip one half of the omelet over the other half, and slide onto a warmed plate.

Optional omelet fillings
- Put filling in a strip in the centre of the just-set omelet, then fold one half over the other half. Use finely chopped cooked vegetables, fish or chicken, etc, warmed first in a microwave oven or sautéed in another pan before adding. OR: sliced mushrooms cooked in a little butter or cream; sautéed bacon or ham; reheated creamed corn; crumbled blue cheese or grated cheddar; chopped, smoked salmon. Sprinkle finely chopped fresh herbs over the omelet before folding it, if desired.

Pizzas

Pizzas make an excellent easy lunch — equally enjoyable hot, cold or reheated. There are many different options but it is really just a matter of tossing a few selected toppings (even a collection of leftovers from the fridge) onto a bought or home-made base (see below), and baking.

For 2 large or 8 individual pizzas
1 quantity Easy Pizza Base (below)
½ cup tomato pizza topping, bought
    or home-made (see method)

Then select 2–3 toppings
a little thinly sliced **onion**
thinly sliced red/green/yellow
    capsicums
sliced **mushrooms**
sliced or diced **ham/bacon**, **salami**,
    sliced cooked **sausages**, shredded
    chicken, assorted **seafood** or
    surimi, etc.
thin slices or wedges of **tomato** (or
    halved **cherry tomatoes**)
chargrilled or roasted vegetables
    (**tomatoes, mushrooms, capsicums,
    eggplant, zucchini, artichoke
    hearts**, etc.)
anchovies and/or chopped **olives**
chopped fresh or dried **basil**,
    thyme, etc.

250–350g sliced, grated, or crumbled
    cheese (mild or tasty cheddar,
    mozzarella, feta, or a mixture)
olive oil to drizzle (optional)

- To make a tomato pizza topping, stir together ½ cup tomato paste, 1 tsp garlic salt, ½ tsp basil or oregano and pepper to taste. Add 2–3 Tbsp water and mix to make an easily spreadable paste.
- Heat the oven to 200°C while you assemble your pizza/s. Place the bases on a lightly oiled (or Teflon-lined) oven slide or pizza tray. Start by spreading the base/s with a thin layer of tomato topping, then add your selection of the suggested toppings (2–3 are generally plenty).
- Top with a generous layer of sliced, grated, or crumbled cheese, and if you like, drizzle lightly with olive oil.
- Bake at 200°C for 10–15 minutes, or until the base has browned underneath.

Easy Pizza Base

Home-made yeasted pizza bases are hard to beat, and are really very easy to prepare, particularly if you have a breadmaker.

**For 1 very large, 2 medium, or 8
individual bases**
3 tsp instant active dried yeast
½ cup milk
¾ cup boiling water
2 tsp sugar
1½ tsp salt
2 Tbsp olive or canola oil
3 cups high grade flour
additional flour or water if required

- If making by hand: Measure the yeast into a large bowl. Combine the milk and water, and add this to the yeast along with the sugar, salt and oil. Leave to stand for a couple of minutes, then add half the flour and stir well to make a thick batter. Add the remaining flour and stir to make a dough firm enough to knead (add extra flour if required). Tip onto a floured surface and knead for 5–10 minutes, then cover the dough loosely and leave to rise for about 10 minutes before using.
- If using a bread machine: Measure all the ingredients into the machine, set the machine to the 'Dough' cycle and press start. Check the dough after a few minutes of mixing. If it looks too wet add a little extra flour, or a little water if too dry. The dough can be removed from the machine any time after about 30 minutes from the start of mixing, but if you have time, let the cycle run through.
- Turn dough onto a floured surface and divide as required, then roll each piece into a thin (5–7mm) round shape.

CORN FRITTERS

Corn Fritters

Who didn't love corn fritters as a kid? We have to admit they're probably not something we'd usually think of serving adults (as a main at least), but if you have a can of corn in the pantry, they can be knocked up in a few minutes. Try them plain, or add some of the extras given below and serve them with tomato sauce or a chunky salsa. They make a delicious meal in minutes — perfect for lunch at the bach.

For 3–4 servings
2 large eggs
½ cup beer (or soda water, milk etc)
½ tsp each salt and pepper
1 cup self-raising flour
410g can whole kernel corn, well
    drained
oil to fry (see method)

Optional extras
1 tsp each cumin and paprika
1–2 spring onions, finely sliced
2–3 Tbsp chopped coriander
1 medium red (or green) capsicum,
    deseeded and diced

- Break the eggs into a medium-sized bowl. Add the beer (or other liquid), salt and pepper, then stir together. Measure in the flour and stir just enough to make a smooth batter.
- Add the corn and any of the optional extras and mix just enough to combine.
- Heat the oil in a large non-stick pan; for corn cakes use just 1–2 Tbsp, or for traditional fritters you will need oil 5–10mm deep. Carefully drop spoonfuls of batter into the pan, cooking in batches for 3–5 minutes per side until golden brown, or until the fritters are lightly browned on both sides and firm when pressed in the centre.
- Drain cooked fritters on several layers of paper towel. Keep cooked fritters or cakes warm in the oven until all the mixture is cooked, then stack them on plates and serve immediately with tomato sauce or your favourite salsa.

Sushi

A platter of several different shapes and varieties of sushi makes a tasty and visually appealing meal.

For 2–3 main servings
1 cup short-grain rice
1¾ cups boiling water
2 Tbsp rice or wine vinegar
2 Tbsp sugar
1 Tbsp sherry
1 tsp salt

Fillings

The fillings you choose will depend on the type of sushi you are making and your own preferences, but here are a few suggestions:
strips of **cucumber**
strips of **carrot**
sliced **avocado**
strips of **red/green/yellow capsicum**
smoked (or raw) **salmon**
strips of **omelet**
shredded **surimi**
fresh (or canned) **tuna**
pickled ginger
pickled vegetables
wasabi paste
yaki nori (roasted seaweed sheets)

- Place the rice in a large container and cover with cold water. Drain the rice, then cover with water and drain again.
- To microwave: Put the rice in a large microwave bowl. Add the boiling water then cover the bowl and microwave at Medium (50%) for 15–20 minutes or until the rice is completely tender. Remove the bowl from the microwave and stir in the vinegar, sugar, sherry and salt. Leave rice to cool to room temperature.
- To cook conventionally: Put the rice in a large heavy pot (with a close-fitting lid), pour in the boiling water, bring rice to the boil, then cover pot and reduce the heat to very low and leave to steam for 15 minutes. Remove the pot from the heat and stand for a further 10 minutes before stirring in the vinegar, sugar, sherry and salt. Leave rice to cool to room temperature.

Rolled Sushi (Maki-sushi)

- Sushi rolls are actually very easy to make. Lay a sheet of nori (seaweed) on a clean dry bench or sushi mat (the mat makes getting the roll started a little easier). Spread a layer of rice about 1cm thick over the nori, leaving a 2–3cm strip down one long edge clear. Arrange selected filling/s along the middle of the rice. Brush the exposed nori with a little water, then roll up starting from the rice-covered edge. Sit the roll seam side down for 2–3 minutes before cutting into 2–3cm thick slices.
- To serve: Arrange your sushi on plates or a platter and serve with pickled ginger, wasabi paste and a bowl of Kikkoman soy sauce for dipping.

Salads

A GOOD SALAD WILL BRIGHTEN ANY MEAL. WE LOVE THE
INTERESTING VARIETY AND THE FACT THAT YOU ARE ABLE TO
CHOOSE A SALAD THAT IS JUST RIGHT FOR ANY SEASON
AND SITUATION.

CAESAR SALAD

Caesar Salad

A good Caesar Salad is really hard to beat — no wonder it is the most popular of the salads! Make sure you use very crisp lettuce leaves. We've stuck to the classic 'plain' version, but it is often now served topped with grilled chicken or even a poached egg.

For 4–6 servings
1 Cos (Romaine) lettuce
1 cup freshly shaved Parmesan cheese
½–1 cup croutons (see method)

Dressing
1 egg
1 clove garlic
juice of 1 lime or lemon
2 anchovy fillets
1 tsp Dijon mustard
about ½ tsp salt
freshly ground black pepper
½ cup extra virgin olive oil

- Separate and wash lettuce leaves; dry well. Chill for several hours, or overnight. Leaves should be cold and dry when the salad is made.
- Make the dressing by combining all the ingredients except the oil in a food processor or blender. Blend until smooth, then, while the motor is still running, pour in the olive oil in a slow steady stream until the dressing is as thick as thickened pouring cream. Taste and adjust the seasonings.
- To assemble the salad, arrange the leaves in a large salad bowl, sprinkling the croutons through them. Just before serving, drizzle the dressing over the leaves and toss to coat lettuce and croutons. Strew with the freshly shaved Parmesan.
- To make croutons: Melt 25g butter and pour over 4 cups cubed stale bread, sprinkle with 1–2 tsp flavoured salt (onion or celery are good). Arrange the bread cubes in a single layer on an oven tray, and put under the grill (at least 10cm away from heat). Grill until lightly browned, turning every few minutes. Extra croutons can be stored in an airtight container for later use.

Leafy Green Salads

Our present-day salads are a far cry from the shredded lettuce salads with condensed milk dressing, made regularly throughout the summer by many of our parents and grandparents 50 years ago!

choose from (or grow) a variety of
    lettuce leaves of different ages, sizes,
    shapes and colours
young spinach leaves
crunchy radish, bean or other sprouts
    of various types
more strongly flavoured greens, such
    as rocket (arugula) and watercress

- Make sure that you wash and dry the salad greens you use before you add dressing to them.
- To dry and chill them, arrange the washed, drained salad greens on a strip of paper towel or on a clean dry teatowel. Roll the towel up like a sponge roll, with the greens inside, then put in large plastic bag, open at one end. Refrigerate for several hours. Just before serving, put the cold, crisp, dried greens into a large salad bowl and toss gently with a small amount of one of the following dressings. (If there is a puddle of dressing in the bottom of the bowl, you have used too much.)

French Dressing

This is a good, all-purpose dressing which you can make in a few minutes, keep in the refrigerator, and shake before use. (Mustard helps to stop dressing from separating.)

¼ cup olive or avocado oil
2 tsp white wine vinegar
1 tsp Dijon or other mixed mustard
¼ tsp salt
1 tsp sugar

- Put all the ingredients in a screw-topped bottle or jar, then shake well. Refrigerate up to a week; shake well before using.

Italian Dressing

- Put all the ingredients for French Dressing in a jar or bottle, then add 1 tsp of tomato paste. Shake, taste, and add another teaspoonful if you want a slightly stronger tomato flavour.

Herbed Dressing

- Make French Dressing without the salt, and add 1–2 Tbsp of very finely chopped fresh herbs such as parsley, chives, dill leaves, tarragon, thyme or rosemary. Replace the salt with herb, garlic, onion or celery salt if you like.

Greek Summer Salad

This summertime salad has stood the test of time! It is great served with barbecued lamb, but it can be a meal in itself if you change the proportions, adding more feta to the vegetables and serving it with generous amounts of crusty bread.

For 4 servings

1 thin-skinned telegraph cucumber, about 30cm long

8 medium-sized ripe, red tomatoes

1 small to medium red onion

dried oregano leaves

50–100g feta cheese

about 20 black olives

¼–½ cup extra virgin olive oil

freshly ground black pepper

1 lemon

- Cut the cucumber in half lengthways, then, using a small teaspoon, scrape out and discard all the central seedy part. Cut the cucumber flesh into slices about 1cm thick and arrange them on four fairly large flat plates.
- Cut each tomato in half lengthways, then cut each half into four quarters. Divide the cubes between the four plates, on top of the cucumber.
- Slice the peeled onion into very thin rounds and separate the rings, then sprinkle them over each plate.
- Take a good pinch of dried oregano for each plate, crumble the leaves between your fingers and sprinkle them over the vegetables.
- Cut the feta into small cubes and divide between the plates, then arrange about 5 black olives attractively over the rest of the salads.
- Just before serving, drizzle 1–2 Tbsp of olive oil over the salads, as well as a little black pepper.
- Halve the lemon and squeeze the juice from both halves over all the salad ingredients.
- Serve slices of crusty bread beside the salads and place 1–2 lamb kebabs on the side of each plate.

NOTE: *Because feta cheese is salty, it is usually not necessary to add salt to the salad or the dressing.*

Waldorf Salad

This lovely crunchy salad is particularly useful when tomatoes and other summer fruits and vegetables are not readily available. We like to add a little curry to the dressing, but it's not essential.

For 2–4 servings

2 crisp red apples

2 Tbsp lemon juice

2–3 stalks of celery

¼–½ cup walnut halves or pieces

1–2 spring onions

2–4 cups roughly chopped iceberg lettuce or other salad leaves

Dressing

1 Tbsp sugar

¼ tsp salt

1 tsp curry powder or curry paste, optional

2 tsp Dijon or other mixed mustard

2 Tbsp each lemon juice, sour cream and canola oil

2–3 Tbsp water or orange juice

- First make the dressing. Mix the first seven ingredients in a medium-sized bowl, then thin the mixture to coating consistency with the water or orange juice. Refrigerate until needed or use immediately.
- A short time before serving, cut the unpeeled apples into wedges or cubes. Put them in a large bowl then sprinkle and toss in the lemon juice.
- Chop the celery in thin slices or 1cm squares and add to the apple. Roughly (not finely) chop the walnuts and finely slice the spring onions. Put most of the walnuts and spring onions in the apple mixture, then toss the mixture together, coating everything with the thinned dressing.
- Pile the apple mixture on the prepared lettuce or salad leaves on individual plates, sprinkle each with the remaining chopped walnuts and spring onions, and serve immediately.

Chicken Waldorf Salad

- Make the salad as above, but add to the apple, celery and dressing mixture, smallish, rather chunky slices of smoked chicken. Use quantities to suit yourself (say 75–100g per person) and serve the salad as a main dish with crusty bread, rather than as a side dish.

GREEK SUMMER SALAD

MOROCCAN CARROT & CUMIN SALAD

Moroccan Carrot & Cumin Salad

So many people indicated that they like carrots, we thought we should include a carrot-based recipe, but were then struck with the thought, 'What should it be?' This recipe is delicious and a little different. It certainly features carrots as the 'hero' so we thought it was a good fit.

For 4 servings

3–4 medium-sized (about 500g total) carrots

2 cloves garlic, peeled and chopped

½ tsp ground coriander seed

½ tsp minced red chilli

½ cup hot water

2 Tbsp lemon juice

2 Tbsp extra virgin olive oil

2 tsp ground cumin

1 tsp honey

½ tsp salt

8–10 pitted Kalamata olives, roughly chopped

¼–½ small red onion, thinly sliced

2–3 Tbsp chopped coriander leaf

- Scrub or peel the carrots, then cut them diagonally into slices 5–7mm thick. Place in a large, lidded pot or frypan, then add the garlic, coriander seed, minced chilli and water. Cover, then bring to the boil and cook for 5 minutes, before removing the lid and cooking for 1–2 minutes longer, or until the water has evaporated.
- Transfer the cooked carrots to a bowl, then add all the remaining ingredients except the chopped coriander leaf. Toss gently to combine. Allow the carrots to cool to room temperature, stirring once or twice, then sprinkle with the chopped coriander and serve. (Alternatively, make the salad in advance and refrigerate for up to 24 hours, letting the salad come to room temperature and adding the coriander before serving.)

American-style Potato Salad

This ever-popular, mildly flavoured salad travels well (although it should be kept cool) and makes a great lunch. It is very good plain, but can also be dressed up by the addition of extras.

For 3–4 servings

1kg waxy or new potatoes

2 Tbsp white wine vinegar

2 Tbsp olive or canola oil

½ cup American-style mayonnaise, bought or home-made (see below)

about 2 Tbsp milk or lemon juice

2 tsp white wine vinegar

2 sticks celery, sliced

2 spring onions, sliced

¼ cup chopped parsley

salt and pepper to taste

- Scrub the potatoes, then boil them gently until just cooked. Drain and return to the cooking pot. Add the first measure of vinegar and the oil. Toss gently to coat and then leave to stand until at room temperature.
- Thin the mayonnaise with the milk or lemon juice and the second measure of vinegar. Slice or cube the cooled potatoes into a large bowl, then add the celery, sliced spring onions, chopped parsley and the mayonnaise mixture (and one or two of the optional extras, if desired). Mix gently, without breaking up the potato too much.
- We like to serve this at about room temperature, but if you're making it in advance, it should be refrigerated until shortly before it is required. Serve as is or garnished with some more parsley and/or chives.

NOTE: *optional extras: chopped hard-boiled egg; sliced frankfurter or bier stick; sliced or chopped gherkins; crispy fried bacon; roasted pumpkin seeds.*

Mayonnaise

Quick and easy to make in the food processor, this sauce is delicious and versatile. It puts most bought mayonnaises to shame!

For about 1 ½ cups

1 egg

2 Tbsp wine vinegar

½ tsp each salt and sugar

1 tsp Dijon or mild mustard

about 1 cup light olive or canola oil

- Measure the first five ingredients into a food processor or blender. Turn on and add the oil in a thin stream until the mayonnaise is as thick and creamy as you like it. Keep in a covered container in the refrigerator for up to 3 weeks.

East-West Beef Salad *with Coriander Dressing*

Asian-style salads seem to have found their way into the hearts and minds (presumably via the stomachs!) of New Zealanders. We can't claim this main-dish salad is completely authentic, but we think it captures the essential flavours and it's certainly delicious.

For 2 servings
200–250g rump steak, cut 2cm thick
1 Tbsp each soy sauce and canola oil
1 Tbsp canola oil
mixed salad leaves
cucumber chunks
cherry tomatoes
sliced cooked green beans
avocado slices
basil leaves

Coriander Dressing
1–2 cloves garlic
1 tsp thinly sliced lemongrass stalk
2 Tbsp sugar
1 Tbsp fish sauce
2 Tbsp each lime juice and water
¼ tsp salt
⅛ tsp chilli powder or minced red chilli
2–3 Tbsp coriander leaf
1 chopped spring onion

- Trim any fat from the steak. Coat steak with a little soy sauce and oil and leave to marinade for at least 15 minutes, or up to 24 hours, in the refrigerator.
- Prepare the salad ingredients, as necessary, making two salads in shallow bowls.
- About 15 minutes before serving, preheat a heavy pan over high heat and pan-grill steak in the dry pan for 1–2 minutes per side until brown on the outside but pink in the middle. Put steak on a carving board and leave to cool.
- To make the dressing, finely chop the garlic and thinly sliced lemongrass in a food processor or blender. Add the remaining dressing ingredients and process until coriander leaves are chopped.
- Just before serving, slice the cooled meat into thin strips and coat with part of the dressing. Arrange slices on the individual salads and drizzle over extra dressing. Serve with crusty bread or with bowls of basmati or jasmine rice.

Thai-style Peanutty Noodle Salad

To make this salad more substantial and a meal on its own, add a little cooked or smoked chicken.

For 4–6 servings
250g fine or ribbon egg noodles
1 large carrot
½ cup whole green beans
½ small cucumber
1–2 spring onions
2 Tbsp lime or lemon juice
chopped fresh chilli, optional

Dressing
3 Tbsp peanut butter
2 tsp sesame oil
1 Tbsp each sherry and brown sugar
2 Tbsp each light soy sauce and
    canola oil
1 clove garlic, minced
2 Tbsp grated fresh ginger
¼ cup hot water
2–3 Tbsp chopped fresh coriander leaf,
    optional
½–1 tsp minced red chilli
salt to taste

- Prepare the dressing by measuring all the ingredients except salt into a screw-top jar and shaking until they are well combined. Add the salt to taste then leave to stand while you prepare the remaining ingredients.
- Cook the noodles until they are just done (over-cooked noodles will be soggy and weak). Drain, then rinse well with cold water. Toss with a little oil and set aside. Cut the carrot into fine strips or matchsticks, and combine with the beans in a shallow pan, cover with water and boil for about 1 minute. Drain and set aside with the noodles.
- Halve the cucumber lengthways, scoop out and discard the seeds, cut the cucumber as you did the carrot. Cut the white section of the spring onion/s lengthways into fine strips (keep the green part for a garnish), and add these to the other vegetables.
- Toss the noodles, vegetables and dressing together in a large bowl. If possible leave to stand for 15–30 minutes, then sprinkle with the lime or lemon juice and toss again. Garnish with chopped spring onion greens and/or fresh red chilli and serve.

EAST-WEST BEEF SALAD

Vegetarian

VEGETARIANS AND MEAT-EATERS ALIKE WILL ENJOY THE RECIPES IN
THIS SECTION. YOU'LL FIND MORE VEGETARIAN RECIPES IN
OTHER PARTS OF THE BOOK — ENJOY THEM ALL!

CREAMY SPINACH, MUSHROOM & BLUE CHEESE RISOTTO

Creamy Spinach, Mushroom & Blue Cheese Risotto

Risottos seem to be very popular with New Zealanders these days. This tasty vegetarian version can be prepared in less than 40 minutes with very little planning.

For 2–3 servings

2 Tbsp olive or canola oil

1 medium onion, diced

2 cloves garlic, chopped

250g mushrooms, sliced

1 tsp dried thyme

1 cup arborio or canarolli rice

2½ cups boiling water

2 tsp instant mushroom stock powder

100g baby spinach leaves

¼ cup cream

50g creamy blue cheese, crumbled

salt and pepper to taste

basil or thyme and a little additional blue cheese or Parmesan to garnish

- Heat the oil in a large non-stick pan. Add the onion and garlic and cook, stirring frequently, until the onion is soft. Stir in the mushrooms and thyme and cook, stirring occasionally, until the mushrooms soften. Add the rice and cook for 2–3 minutes longer, stirring constantly.
- Add 1 cup of hot water and the instant stock powder. Bring to the boil, then reduce the heat and cook, stirring frequently, until the liquid has almost disappeared. Add the remaining water half a cup at a time, simmering and stirring frequently until the liquid has almost gone before making the next addition. After about 20 minutes, test to see if the rice is cooked (grains should be firm but with no hard centres). Add another ¼–½ cup water and simmer for a few minutes longer if necessary. When the rice is cooked, stir in the spinach leaves, add the cream and sprinkle in the blue cheese. Stir gently to combine. Season to taste with salt and pepper.
- Heat through, then serve immediately, garnished with a little basil or thyme and some additional crumbled blue cheese or shaved or grated Parmesan, if you like. A simple green or tomato salad, some crusty bread and a glass of wine make ideal accompaniments.

Chickpea, Spinach & Potato Curry

This makes a great vegetarian meal, easy and delicious on its own, but even more interesting when served with an array of Indian condiments.

For 4 large servings

2 Tbsp canola oil

1 large onion, diced

2 cloves garlic, crushed, peeled and chopped

1 Tbsp finely chopped ginger

2–3 medium (about 300g) waxy potatoes, cut into 1cm cubes

2–3 tsp curry powder (mild or hot to taste)

½–1 tsp cumin seeds, optional

2–3 bay leaves

250g package frozen spinach, thawed

400g can whole tomatoes in juice

310–400g can chickpeas, drained

¼–½ cup water, if required

2 tsp garam masala

salt and pepper to taste

2 Tbsp chopped fresh coriander

- Heat the oil in a large pot. Add the onion, garlic and ginger and stir-fry until the onion has softened and is turning clear. Add the potatoes, curry powder, cumin seeds (if using), and the bay leaves. Cook for 1–2 minutes then add the spinach with its liquid and the tomatoes in juice. Crush the tomatoes, then stir in the chickpeas.
- Gently simmer for 15 minutes or until the potato cubes are tender, adding a little water if the mixture begins to look dry. When the potatoes are cooked, add the garam masala and season to taste with salt and pepper. Add the chopped coriander.
- For a simple meal serve in bowls as is. Alternatively serve with rice, naan bread or poppadums, and assorted chutneys and relishes.

Spinach & Feta Pie

This very simple pie is loosely based on Greek spanakopita — it is another great example of how filo pastry can be used to make a dramatic-looking dish with a minimum amount of effort. It can be served hot, warm or cold and is great as part of a summer picnic.

For 4–6 servings

1 Tbsp olive oil

1 medium onion, diced

¼ cup pine nuts

500g frozen spinach, thawed and drained

200g feta cheese, crumbled

¼ tsp dried basil

¼ tsp thyme

¼–½ tsp freshly grated nutmeg

½–1 tsp salt

black pepper to taste

2 eggs

10 sheets filo pastry

about 2 Tbsp melted butter or olive oil

- Heat the oil in a medium-sized pan, add the onion and cook until softened. Stir in the pine nuts and continue to cook until these are golden brown.
- While the onion cooks, squeeze as much liquid as you can from the thawed spinach. Place the spinach in a large bowl and add the crumbled cheese, then the seasonings and the onion and pine nut mixture (the quantity of salt required will depend on the saltiness of the feta — vary it to taste). Add the eggs and stir until well mixed.
- Heat oven to 200°C, and non-stick spray or oil a shallow casserole dish (about 20 x 25cm). Lay 2 sheets of filo out on the bench, and brush the top sheet lightly with melted butter or olive oil. Lay these sheets lengthways down the prepared dish, gently pressing them into the bottom, leaving the over-hanging edges intact. Prepare another 2 sheets and lay these in the dish at right angles to the first sheets. Repeat this process so that there are 8 sheets of filo in the dish.
- Gently spread the spinach filling mix over the pastry in the bottom of the dish. Cover the spinach mixture with another two sheets of filo, folded to make them fit. Fold in the over-hanging edges of the bottom sheets, and lightly brush the surface with oil or melted butter.
- Bake at 200°C for 20–25 minutes until golden brown and firm when pressed in the centre. Serve hot, warm or even cold.

NOTE: *If you would rather, you can use the filling mixture to make 10–12 smaller filo triangles. Lay 1 sheet of filo on a dry surface and brush it lightly with oil, then fold in lengthways in half. Place about ¼ cup of the filling mixture close to one end, then fold the corner up diagonally to cover the filling (so the bottom edge meets the side). Keep folding the filling (straight, then diagonally) until you reach the end of the strip. Fold any extra pastry under the package, brush lightly with oil or melted butter and place on a baking tray. Repeat until all the filling is used. Bake as above, but reduce cooking time to 12–15 minutes.*

Macaroni Cheese

If you're hankering for warming comfort food, it doesn't get much better than this!

For 4–6 servings

400–500g macaroni or spirals

3 Tbsp butter

3 Tbsp flour

¼ tsp grated nutmeg

½ tsp salt

2 cups milk

1 tsp mild mustard (optional)

2 cups (200g) grated cheese, either cheddar, Gruyère or half and half

Optional topping

½–1 cup grated cheese, preferably Gruyère, or ½ cup fresh breadcrumbs mixed with 2 Tbsp melted butter

- Bring a large pot of lightly salted water to a rapid boil, then add the pasta and cook for 8–10 minutes or until tender through.
- While the pasta cooks, melt the butter in a medium-sized pot. Stir in the flour and cook for 1–2 minutes, stirring continuously to remove lumps and prevent browning. Add the nutmeg and salt, then begin adding the milk, half a cup at a time. Stir briskly to break up any lumps and allow the sauce to thicken and boil between each addition. When all the milk has been added and the sauce has returned to the boil, remove it from the heat.
- Add the mustard and the grated cheese, stirring until the cheese has melted and the sauce is smooth and creamy.
- Drain the cooked pasta and stir in the sauce.
- Serve as is, or transfer to an oven-proof dish and top with the additional grated cheese or a breadcrumb mixture. Place under a preheated grill until the top bubbles and/or turns golden brown. Serve and enjoy!

SPINACH & FETA PIE

Vegetable Lasagne

Mixtures of savoury foods layered between lasagne sheets have become so popular in recent years that they are now considered part of our basic cuisine.

For 6 servings

1 Tbsp olive oil

1 onion, finely chopped

1 clove garlic, finely chopped

about 300g mushrooms, sliced

1 tsp fresh thyme, finely chopped

1 cup vegetable stock

1 Tbsp cornflour

¼ cup water

salt and pepper to taste

300g broccoli or spinach, chopped

1 cup (250g) cottage cheese

2 eggs

1 cup grated tasty cheese

salt and pepper to taste

250g fresh lasagne sheets

425g can diced or Italian seasoned
   tomatoes

½ cup grated tasty cheese

- For the first layer: Heat the oil in a large pan, add the onion and garlic and cook until soft but not browned. Stir in the mushrooms and thyme, and cook for 5 minutes more, stirring occasionally. Add the vegetable stock, then thicken the mixture by adding the cornflour mixed with ¼ cup water and heating to boiling. Season to taste with salt and pepper.
- For the second layer: Cook the chopped broccoli or spinach until barely tender, then drain well. Mix the cottage cheese, eggs, grated cheese, and salt and pepper together in a medium-sized bowl. Add the drained broccoli or spinach and stir to combine.
- To assemble: Non-stick spray the inside of a 20 x 30cm casserole dish. Cover the bottom with a layer of lasagne sheets. Spread the mushroom mixture over the lasagne, then cover this with a second layer of lasagne sheets. Spoon the cottage cheese mixture over this, and cover with more lasagne. Pour the canned tomato evenly over the top, covering it completely. Sprinkle with the grated cheese.
- Cover and bake at 180°C for about 40–45 minutes. Remove cover and bake for about 15 minutes longer, until the top is lightly browned.
- Serve with a salad and crusty bread on the side.

Creamy Cheese Quiche

This popular quiche is enjoyed by young and old alike. Although it is at its best when served warm from the oven, it can be made ahead, refrigerated then warmed through in a regular oven or in a microwave oven.

For 4–6 servings

Crust

1 cup flour, preferably high grade

60g very cold butter

3–4 Tbsp cold water

Filling

1 medium to large onion, thinly sliced

about 1 tsp canola or other oil

1 cup grated medium, or tasty,
   cheddar

2 large eggs

½ cup milk plus ½ cup cream, or 1 cup
   evaporated milk

- Heat the oven to 220°C, with a rack just above the middle.
- Measure the flour into a food processor bowl. Add the cold butter, cut into 9 cubes and process in bursts, with a metal chopping blade, until the butter pieces are pea-sized. Add the cold water gradually, processing briefly in bursts, until the dough forms a ball. Refrigerate the ball of dough for a few minutes.
- Meantime, slice the onion thinly into rings, and sauté over low to medium heat, in a covered frying pan in the oil, until just tender, separating the rings as they cook.
- Roll the chilled pastry out to fit a 23cm pie plate or a 23cm flan dish with a removable bottom. Without stretching the pastry, line the container with it, then trim the edges.
- Spread the onion rings evenly in the quiche, and sprinkle with grated cheese.
- Process the eggs, milk and cream (or evaporated milk) in the unwashed processor bowl until mixed but not foamy, then pour into the pastry-lined tin.
- Bake at 220°C for 10 minutes, then at 180°C for 15–20 minutes, until the filling has set in the centre. Cool for about 10 minutes, then serve in wedges, with a salad and crusty bread.

VARIATION: *For a non-vegetarian Quiche Lorraine, add 3 rashers of chopped, sautéed bacon. Cook the onion in the bacon fat, and replace the grated cheddar with 100g sliced Gruyère cheese.*

Seafood

IT COULD BE EASY TO THINK THAT KIWIS OFTEN TAKE THEIR BEAUTIFUL BEACHES, SPARKLING SEAS AND THE WIDE VARIETY OF DELICIOUS SEAFOOD THEY CAN CATCH OR BUY AND ENJOY REGULARLY FOR GRANTED — BUT THEY DON'T!

OLD-FASHIONED FISH PIE

Old-fashioned Fish Pie

Fish pie is delicious — it is also our most popular fish dish. Perhaps the 'comfort food' factor comes into play, but it's amazing just how enthusiastically it is received.

For 4 servings

about 750g potatoes

2 eggs

2 leeks (about 600g), trimmed and
    sliced 1cm thick

3 Tbsp butter

300–450g can smoked fish or salmon

½ tsp curry powder

2 Tbsp flour

1½ cups liquid (see method)

milk for mashed potatoes

- Peel the potatoes, then boil them in plenty of lightly salted boiling water until tender. Add the eggs to the potatoes as they cook and boil them for 12–15 minutes. Lift the eggs out and cool them under cold water, then chop or slice them. Drain the cooked potatoes and set aside.
- Place the leeks in a pot with 1 Tbsp of butter and ¼ cup water, cover and cook for about 5 minutes, then drain, reserving the liquid.
- Drain the canned fish, adding the liquid to the reserved leek water. Mix the fish, leeks and chopped hard-boiled eggs together in a lightly buttered or non-stick sprayed 18 x 23cm ovenware dish.
- Make the reserved fish-leek liquid up to 1½ cups with milk. Heat the remaining butter, curry powder and flour in a medium-sized pot (use the same pot you cooked the leeks in) until bubbling. Add half the liquid and stir until boiling. Add remaining liquid and boil again, stirring constantly, then simmer for 4–5 minutes. Mix the sauce through the fish mixture.
- Mash the potatoes with milk until creamy, then beat with a fork. Spoon the potato over the fish mixture, roughen the surface with a fork and sprinkle with a little Parmesan cheese. (The pie can be made ahead to this point and refrigerated until required.)
- Bake at 175°C until potato topping is lightly browned, about 20 minutes if just prepared, or 30–45 minutes if made ahead and refrigerated.

Pan-fried Fish Fillets

Aren't we lucky to have the sea 'at our doorstep' — almost all New Zealand children have sat in the sun on a wharf, with a line and baited hook, and think of all the older New Zealanders who find very good reasons to 'go fishing' instead of mowing the lawn at the weekend! Pan-fried fish fillets are delicious, and easy to cook. This particular recipe has been our basic fried fish recipe for as long as we can remember.

- Choose fillets of your favourite fish. Cut the fillets into pieces of more or less even shape. If there are rows of bones in the fish, try to cut them out during this process.
- In a shallow bowl mix an egg with 2 Tbsp of milk and about ½ tsp salt. Add small amounts of other flavourings such as curry powder or paprika to the egg and milk mixture, if you like. Place about 1 cup of self-raising or plain flour (we prefer self-raising flour) in another shallow container, or on a large piece of baking paper.
- Heat a large frying pan containing oil 2–3mm deep. Turn the oven on so that plates can be heated and the fillets that are cooked first can be kept warm.
- Working with one fillet at a time, coat each side with the flour, then pat off the excess. Dip it into the seasoned egg so both sides are coated. Turn the egg-coated fillet in the dry flour again then place it gently in the hot oil in the frypan.
- Repeat, adding each fillet to the pan as it is coated, and turning each fillet when its first side is cooked. Unless the fillets are very thick, the fish should be cooked by the time the coating on each side is golden brown. (Make more coating and add extra oil to the pan as needed.)
- Serve with lemon wedges and cooked vegetables, or salad.

VARIATION: *Instead of dipping the fish fillets in the flour for a second time, dip it first in flour, then in egg, then in fine dry breadcrumbs. The crumbs make a thicker coating and produce a brighter golden brown coating.*

NOTE: *You get a thicker and more even coating by dipping the fish in flour before it is dipped in egg, so it doesn't pay to omit this step.*

Sesame Steamed Fish

Whole fish are sometimes too big to fit in a pan on top of the stove, and although you can bake them, this may take longer. Both whole fish and fish fillets microwave very successfully, so it's well worth trying. This recipe gives the fish a delicious oriental flavour.

For 4 servings
1 whole fish (600–700g)
3–4 spring onions
2cm length of root ginger
2 Tbsp Kikkoman soy sauce
1 Tbsp sesame oil

- Select a microwave-proof platter large enough to hold the fish with its head intact. (If it is a little too big, cut off the tail and microwave it separately on High for 30 seconds, then put it back in place for serving, with a garnish over the scar.)
- Check the fish has its scales removed and is gutted. Slash the thickest part of each side with several parallel cuts.
- Cut the spring onions into 2cm lengths, then cut them and the ginger into matchsticks. Mix the soy sauce and the sesame oil and brush evenly over the fish and inside the body cavity. Put half the ginger and onion under the fish and the rest on top. Cover the fish with microwave-proof cling film, tucking the edges under the dish.
- Microwave on High for 50 seconds per 100g of fish. Leave to stand, still covered with wrap, for 4 minutes, then check to see if the flesh in the thickest part looks opaque and will flake. If not, microwave it for 1–2 minutes longer, and check again. Repeat if necessary.
- To serve, lift the flesh off the bone, and spoon over some juices.

VARIATIONS:
- Just before serving heat 1 Tbsp of extra sesame oil and spoon over the fish.
- Use the same ingredients, but replace the whole fish with boned, skinned fillets. Grate the ginger and chop the onion more finely if desired. Allow the same cooking time per 100g.
- To bake conventionally: Proceed as above, placing the fish on a double layer of foil (extra-wide foil is great) big enough to fold into a package that will completely enclose the fish. This is better than a platter. Carefully fold up and seal the foil package. Bake at 180°C for about 12 minutes per 500g fish.
- To barbecue: Foil wrap the fish as for baking, then place on a barbecue and turn every 5 minutes. The only way to know if the fish is cooked is to open the package every now and then and check. The flesh at the thickest part will flake when the fish is cooked.

Stir-fried Paua

The underside of a paua shell is beautifully coloured, but the tough, hard, muscular foot inside this shell looks very uninviting by comparison. If you are starting with paua in their shells, you should prise the flesh from the shell, discard everything except the muscular foot and the dark frilly part around it, and cut out and discard the hard mouthpart from one edge.

- Views vary concerning scrubbing and pounding the foot, but we have found that the end result can be excellent without either of these processes if the fleshy foot is cut into very thin slices (2–3mm) with a really sharp knife. (We have not cooked frozen, sliced paua, but have been told that it is not particularly good.)
- A few minutes before you are ready to eat the paua (as a starter course) heat a large, heavy frying pan, add about 1 Tbsp of butter and some finely chopped garlic. As soon as it's melted, add the thin slices of one or two paua and stir fry. The paua will be at its most tender just after it has been heated through. Add a little lemon juice, some pepper and a dash of salt or light soy sauce, garnish with finely chopped chives or spring onion and serve immediately with crusty bread.

Beer-battered Fish Fingers

Fish and chips are part of our New Zealand heritage. They are popular with everyone and I'm sure anyone could tell you where their favourite fish and chip shop is. This recipe is one we have used for years, and the results are often served alongside home-made chips or wedges (see page 72).

For 4 servings
600–700g boneless fish fillets
canola or other oil for frying
1 large egg
½ cup of beer or lager
1 Tbsp oil
½ tsp salt
½ tsp curry powder, optional
½ cup plain or self-raising flour

NOTE: *Consider buying a deep fat fryer if you make these regularly. Decide which flour you like best in the batter, then stick with it!*

- Cut the fish fillets into strips about 2cm wide and about 5cm long. Put the pieces on a paper towel to keep them dry. (Cutting the fillets into fingers ensures that there is plenty of crisp coating, and the smaller pieces of fish cook more quickly.)
- Heat 4–7cm of oil in a high-sided frying pan.
- Mix the batter in a fairly shallow bowl. Beat egg, beer, oil, and salt with a fork until well mixed. Add the curry powder and flour, mixed together, then sprinkle over the liquids. Fold everything together until there are no lumps, trying to avoid mixing more than is necessary.
- When the oil is hot but not smoking, drop in a little batter. If it browns in a couple of minutes, dip the fish fingers, one at a time, into dry flour, then into the batter, until coated. The batter should be thick enough to coat the fish thinly. If it is too thick, add extra beer — if it is too thin, stir in more flour. Carefully lower the fish fingers, one at a time, into the pan. Cook several pieces of fish at a time, turning with tongs as necessary. Don't let any liquids drop into the hot oil, and keep children out of the way in case there are any spatters.
- By the time the batter on each finger is golden brown, the fish inside will be cooked. Drain on kitchen paper, keep warm in a warming drawer or serve as soon as each batch is cooked.

Oyster Fritters

Many older New Zealanders think longingly of the days when oysters were considerably cheaper and could be enjoyed, simply and traditionally, straight from the half shell, on lightly buttered brown bread, with a squeeze of lemon juice. Oyster fritters, however, make a pottle of oysters go considerably further, and are very popular.

For 2 large or 3 medium-sized servings
Canola or other flavourless oil for frying
1 pottle (200 ml) of whole, 'cut' or
    small oysters
the liquid from the oysters made up to
    ¼ cup with milk, if necessary
2 eggs
½ tsp salt
a dash of Kaitaia Fire, Tabasco™ or
    other hot chilli sauce, optional
1 cup self-raising flour

- Heat a frypan containing canola or other flavourless oil, 1cm deep, to low-medium heat. Tip the oysters into a sieve above a bowl, saving the liquid that drains from them. Measure the liquid and make it up to ¼ cup with milk if necessary. Leave the oysters whole, or chop them into smaller pieces for maximum flavour and to make them go further.
- In a large, preferably fairly shallow bowl, beat the eggs, salt, Tabasco and the oyster liquid mixture together with a fork until well mixed. Sift in the self-raising flour and stir together until no lumps of flour are visible. (Don't mix any more than necessary.) Add the prepared oysters and fold into the batter, again without over-mixing.
- To check that the oil is the right temperature, drop a ½ tsp of the batter into the pan. If it sizzles and darkens slightly, it is hot enough. If it sizzles and browns straight away, let it cool before starting.
- Use a dessertspoon to lift a single batter-coated oyster from the bowl, helping it off the spoon, into the hot oil, with a second spoon. OR put a spoonful of the chopped oyster mixture into the pan in the same way. If the batter seems too thick to spoon easily, stir in a little more milk. If it is too thin to form fritters, stir in a little extra flour.
- Cook several fritters at once, turning them over with tongs when the underside of each fritter is golden brown. Keep the cooked fritters hot on a paper towel in a shallow container in a low oven. Serve with lemon wedges.

BEER-BATTERED FISH FINGERS

GRILLED OR BARBECUED BACON-WRAPPED SCALLOPS

Grilled or Barbecued Bacon-wrapped Scallops

Scallops are always a treat. Hand them round as a starter, or serve them, several per skewer, as a main part of a casual outdoors summer meal. For a great variation, try using half scallops and half button mushrooms on your skewers.

- It is best to wrap scallops in shaved streaky bacon, since it cooks quickly, ensuring that the scallops are not overcooked. Wood-smoked shaved bacon has a very good flavour.
- A 180g packet of shaved bacon contains about 12 thin slices. Use these to wrap 12 scallops, or you can cut the strips in half crossways and wrap 24 scallops (or 12 scallops and 12 button mushrooms).
- Sprinkle the scallops with a little lemon juice and freshly ground black pepper. If you are wrapping button mushrooms as well, toss them in a shallow bowl containing a little lemon juice, oil, garlic salt and pepper. Carefully separate the bacon strips and lie them flat. Halve them if you like. (This requires some dexterity, time and care.)

- Wrap a strip of bacon around each scallop (or mushroom) and thread alternately on the skewers. Always push the skewer through the end of the bacon strip to stop it unrolling as it cooks.
- Cover with cling film and refrigerate (up to a few hours) until you cook them.
- Cook close to a preheated grill or on a barbecue rack (in preference to a barbecue plate) until the bacon is lightly browned, then turn and brown the other side. (Long cooking overcooks, shrinks and toughens scallops.)
- When serving the scallops (and mushrooms) as starters, gently slide them from the skewers and push a toothpick into each one.

Whitebait Puffs

Henry, Simon's grandfather, used to tell stories of the days when he caught whitebait in the knotted sleeves of a shirt, took them home and, believe it or not, fed them to the pigs! Although these days are now long gone, these light, airy, little fritters capture the distinctive flavour of whitebait and make a little go a long way.

For about 20 puffs

225g (about 1 cup) whitebait, fresh or thawed
2 large eggs, separated
½ tsp salt
1 Tbsp lemon juice
¼ cup self-raising flour
pepper to taste
canola of other oil to cook

- Put a large, fairly heavy non-stick pan on to heat.
- Put the whitebait in a sieve, run cold water through them briefly, then leave to drain. Pick out any pieces of water weed, etc.
- Break the eggs, putting the whites in a small bowl, and the yolks in a large bowl. Add the salt to the whites and beat until they form peaks with tips which turn over at the top when the beater is lifted from them.
- Mix the lemon juice with the yolks, add about a quarter of the beaten whites to make an easier-to-mix batter, then add the flour and stir until mixed in. Add the drained whitebait, then fold everything together. (Do not beat and break up the fish.) Add pepper to taste.
- Drizzle 1 Tbsp of oil into the hot pan, tilt the pan so the bottom is covered, then drop dessertspoonfuls of mixture into the pan, helping the mixture off the end of the spoon with another spoon.
- Cook until bubbles start to burst on the upper side of the puffs, then using a fork to stop the puffs sliding away, turn them over with a stirrer or turner with a thin, flexible blade. Cook the second side until it looks like the first side, then transfer to a plate in a warm oven until all the puffs are cooked. If the puffs are not light brown, turn the heat up or down when you cook the second batch in the same way, after adding a little more oil if necessary.
- Because the puffs are soft and perhaps difficult to pick up with fingers, place one or two (overlapping) on circles or ovals of French bread, or crustless rectangles of Vogel's bread. Add dill or another herb and small lemon wedges for garnish, if you like. Serve as soon as possible after cooking.

Half-shell Mussels with Crunchy Crumb Topping

For 2–4 servings

1.5–2kg fresh mussels

2–3 thick slices of bread

1 clove garlic, peeled

2–3 Tbsp roughly chopped parsley

¼–½ tsp salt

1–2 Tbsp olive oil

- Place the mussels in a large pot or pan with a close-fitting lid. Add about 1cm of hot water then place over a high heat. Cover and allow to come to the boil. Cook for 2–3 minutes, stir once, then cover again and cook for a further 2–3 minutes before removing from the heat. Discard any mussels that have not opened. (Alternatively, place the mussels on the preheated hotplate of a barbecue, cook for about 5 minutes, rearranging them occasionally. Discard any that haven't opened.)
- Allow the mussels to cool until they can be handled, then remove the empty half of the shell.
- Put the roughly torn bread (stale bread works well for this recipe) into a food processor to make coarse crumbs. Add the garlic, parsley and salt and process again until evenly mixed. With the processor running, drizzle in just enough oil to make the crumbs look moist.
- Arrange the half-shell mussels on an oven tray and sprinkle each with 1–2 tsp of the crumbs.
- Place tray 5–10cm below a preheated grill and cook until the crumbs are golden brown and crispy. Arrange on a platter or plates and serve.

Crayfish (Rock Lobster)

These days, for many of us, crayfish are just an occasional treat, but Alison fondly remembers a different time. Her father would regularly stop at Johnson's fish shop in Dunedin and pick up a couple of crays from the pile in the window for just 15 cents each!

- Crayfish are usually bought already boiled, during which process their shells turn from brownish green to bright red. The easiest way to get the flesh from a smallish crayfish is to sit it on a board, back up, with the tail tucked under it, then to cut it in half lengthways. You may find it easier to pull the tail off a large crayfish and halve the tail alone. It is then easy to remove the halved tail meat in one piece and chop it crossways into neat pieces. These can be seasoned with a little lemon juice, pepper and salt, arranged back in the tail shell and served on a flat plate with a herb garnish, bread roll and perhaps a small tomato and cucumber salad alongside.
- Crayfish legs make a good garnish, and like the rest of the body, yield quite a lot of flesh if an enthusiast is prepared to attack them with pliers or strong cutters.
- These are the various yields from a raw crayfish which we cooked, then dismembered and weighed. The raw, whole crayfish weighed 750g. The cooking time, in just enough boiling water to cover it, was 12 minutes. The cooked tail meat weighed 300g. The flesh picked from the tailless body weighed 180g.
- Here are some other suggestions for using crayfish. Take care not to use sauces, oil or dressings which mask the crayfish flavour. Be especially careful when using mayonnaise.
- Try a soured cream mixture with crayfish in rolled bread (like asparagus rolls) or in small filled rolls.
- Mix together, then beat until thick 2 tsp white wine vinegar or lemon juice, ¼ tsp salt, ⅛ tsp each ground pepper, paprika and mustard (optional), 1 tsp sugar and ¼ cup cream. OR try seasoning plain Greek yoghurt or sour cream in the same way, but without the vinegar or lemon juice.
- Make Crayfish Mornay for 2 servings by folding the chopped flesh from a 400g crayfish through cheese sauce, then reheating it carefully, without overcooking.
- To make the cheese sauce, stir together in a medium-sized pot 1 Tbsp each of butter and flour. Add ¼ cup of milk and bring to the boil, stirring all the time, then add ¼ cup of good white wine (e.g. dry Riesling) or extra milk and stir again over low heat until it thickens. Add ½–1 cup of grated tasty cheddar, and fold the prepared crayfish pieces through the sauce. Spoon this into the halved tail shell, into scallop shells or other small containers. Warm through, browning the surface under a hot grill if you like.

HALF-SHELL MUSSELS WITH CRUNCHY CRUMB TOPPING

Chicken

LEMON-GARLIC ROASTED CHICKEN WITH VEGETABLES

Lemon-garlic Roasted Chicken & Vegetables

Roast chicken topped our list of popular chicken recipes! A roast chicken with all the trimmings always seems really special. This version is a favourite of ours for two reasons: it tastes particularly good and it's really easy.

For 4–6 servings

1 chicken, about 1.5–1.8kg
1 large or 2 small lemons
3–4 cloves garlic
2–3 sprigs each fresh thyme and
   tarragon (or rosemary)
1–2 Tbsp olive oil
salt and pepper
1–1.5kg roasting vegetables, e.g.
   floury potatoes, kumara, parsnip,
   pumpkin, red/green/yellow
   capsicums etc.
2–3 Tbsp olive oil
1–2 cloves garlic, extra
3–4 sprigs fresh thyme and tarragon or
   rosemary, optional

- Heat the oven to 200°C. Rinse the chicken inside and out, removing any giblets etc, then pat it dry. Pierce the lemon/s about six times with a sharp knife, then crush and peel the first quantity of garlic. Place the lemon and garlic inside the chicken with the fresh herbs.
- Place the chicken, breast side up, in a large roasting bag and add the olive oil. Season with salt and pepper. Massage the bag so the whole chicken is coated with the oil, then tie the bag, leaving a finger-sized gap at the opening for the steam to escape. Place the bag in a large roasting pan and transfer to the oven to start cooking while you prepare the vegetables.
- Scrub or peel the root vegetables, depending on your preference, then halve or quarter them lengthways depending on their size. Cut the pumpkin into 4–5cm chunks and deseed and quarter the peppers. Crush, peel and chop the second quantity of garlic. Place all the prepared vegetables in a large unpunctured plastic bag, add the oil and toss to coat.
- Remove the vegetables from the bag and arrange them, except the peppers, in the pan around the bagged chicken or in another roasting pan. Add the peppers 20–30 minutes later as they require less time to roast.
- After about 1¼–1½ hours, carefully remove the roasting pan from the oven. If the vegetables have not browned sufficiently, place them under the grill for a few minutes.
- Snip a corner of the oven bag and collect any juices to make gravy (see below), then slit open the whole bag with a sharp knife and pierce the thickest part of the thigh with a sharp knife to check if the chicken is cooked — the juices should run clear, not pink.
- Carve or break up the chicken as required and arrange the meat and vegetables on a warmed platter or serving plates.

Gravy

2 Tbsp flour
2 Tbsp olive oil
1–1½ cups chicken juices, stock,
   water or white wine
salt and pepper to taste

- Measure the flour and oil into a non-stick frypan and mix to a smooth paste. Cook over a high heat until the mixture begins to colour, then gradually add the liquid and stir continuously, to prevent lumps forming, until the gravy boils and thickens. Season to taste with salt and pepper.

CREAMY CHICKEN FETTUCCINE

Creamy Chicken Fettuccine

Pasta is another food that has recently become one of our firm 'everyday' (or even comfort) favourite foods.

For 4–6 servings

400–500g fresh or dried fettuccine

2–3 tsp olive or canola oil

500–600g boneless, skinless chicken breasts or thighs

1 Tbsp flour

2 Tbsp canola oil, extra

2 cloves garlic, peeled and chopped

150g mushrooms, sliced

½ tsp each dried thyme and basil

¾ cup cream

½ cup chicken stock (or ½ cup hot water plus 1 tsp instant chicken stock powder)

½–1 cup frozen peas

½–1 tsp salt, to taste

black pepper

grated Parmesan and a little chopped basil to garnish (optional)

- Heat a large pot of water for the pasta. When the water is boiling, cook the pasta according to the packet instructions. Drain well, then return the pasta to the cooking pot and toss with the oil.
- Cut the chicken across the grain into strips about 1cm wide. Sprinkle these with the flour and toss to combine.
- Heat 1 Tbsp of the extra oil in a large frypan, add the floured chicken and stir-fry for 3–4 minutes until the chicken has lost its pink colour. Transfer the chicken to a bowl.
- Add the remaining oil to the pan, then the garlic and mushrooms. Cook, stirring occasionally, until the mushrooms have softened, then add the herbs, cream and stock. Allow the mixture to come to the boil, stirring occasionally, then add the chicken and any juices. Simmer for 3–4 minutes longer, then stir in the frozen peas, salt and pepper to taste.
- Cook for 2–3 minutes longer, or until the chicken is cooked through. (Cut a piece through the middle: if there's no pink in the centre, it's done.)
- Pour the sauce over the cooked, drained pasta and toss gently to combine. Leave to stand for 2–3 minutes, then stir again and serve, garnishing with a little grated Parmesan and/or chopped fresh basil if desired. Serve as is, or with a salad and crusty bread on the side.

Crispy Coated Chicken Strips

This is our version of oven-baked 'fried' chicken. As you are already using the oven, why not cook some potato wedges at the same time?

For 4 servings

800g–1kg skinless boneless chicken breasts or thighs

½ cup flour

1 tsp garlic salt

1 large egg

1 Tbsp water

1 cup cornflakes, crushed

2 slices bread, crumbed (about 1 cup)

2 tsp paprika

1 tsp curry powder

1–2 Tbsp olive or other oil

- Preheat the oven to 200°C. While the oven heats, cut each chicken breast or thigh lengthways into 2–3 strips (depending on original size), then set aside.
- Coating the chicken is done in three stages, so prepare these mixtures before you proceed any further. Measure the flour and garlic salt into a large plastic bag and shake to combine. Whisk the egg and water together in a flat shallow bowl (a dessert or soup plate works well). Measure the cornflakes into another (medium-sized) plastic bag and crush them lightly with your hands — you don't want them too big, but you don't want to reduce them to dust either. Add the breadcrumbs, paprika and curry powder and shake the bag until well mixed.
- Working 1–2 strips at a time, drop the chicken into the flour mixture and toss the bag until evenly coated. Shake off excess flour and arrange the chicken pieces on a dry surface, repeat until all chicken is floured. Again working 1–2 strips at a time, dip floured chicken pieces into the egg mixture, turning to coat evenly, then drop them into the bag of crumbs, and gently shake until evenly coated.
- Arrange the crumbed chicken in a large non-stick, Teflon or baking paper-lined roasting dish or sponge roll tin and drizzle lightly with the oil. Bake for 12–15 minutes or until golden brown and the thickest piece is no longer pink in the middle when cut through.
- Serve with potato wedges (see page 72) and coleslaw.

Butter Chicken

Butter chicken must be one of the most popular dishes in Indian restaurants — the combination of chicken and a creamy, spiced tomato sauce really is delicious. Our version may not be completely authentic, but it's easy and tastes great.

For 2–3 servings

2 Tbsp canola oil

1 medium onion, finely diced

2 cloves garlic, crushed, peeled and chopped

2 tsp curry powder (mild or hot according to taste)

1 tsp each ground cumin, coriander and ginger

250–300g boneless skinless chicken breasts or thighs, cubed

425g can whole or diced tomatoes in juice

1 Tbsp tomato paste

½ cup evaporated milk or cream

2 tsp garam masala

1–2 tsp honey (optional)

1–2 Tbsp chopped coriander

¼ cup plain unsweetened yoghurt

½–1 tsp salt

- Heat the oil in a large pan, then add the finely diced onion and chopped garlic. Cook, stirring frequently, until the onion is soft and clear but has not browned (about 5 minutes). Add the curry powder, cumin, coriander and ginger, and cook, stirring constantly, for about a minute longer.
- Add the chicken to the pan and cook, stirring occasionally, until it has lost its pinkness, then stir in the canned tomatoes (plus juice), tomato paste and the evaporated milk or cream. Allow the mixture to boil, then reduce the heat to a gentle simmer and cook for 8–10 minutes, or until the chicken is cooked through. (Test by cutting a big piece in half and checking there's no pink in the middle.)
- Stir in the remaining ingredients, add salt to taste, and reheat without boiling. Serve over steamed rice, accompanied with poppadums and/or naan bread. (Naan is now available frozen in many supermarkets.)

VARIATION: *For an extra smooth sauce, try replacing the can of tomatoes with a 410g can of condensed tomato soup.*

Thai-style Green Chicken Curry

It's not so long ago that making a dish like this would have involved a trip to a specialist Asian grocery. These days, curry pastes, and even kaffir lime leaves, are now available from most larger supermarkets — something of a testament to the way New Zealanders have embraced 'new' flavours from Asia.

For 3–4 servings

2 Tbsp canola oil

2 Tbsp Thai green curry paste

1 medium onion, sliced

1 medium potato, cut into 1cm cubes

3–4 kaffir lime leaves, cut into strips about 1cm wide (optional)

300–400g boneless skinless chicken thighs or breasts, cubed

¾ cup coconut cream

2–3 zucchini, sliced

½ cup peas or green beans, fresh or frozen

150–200g can bamboo shoots, drained (optional)

¼–½ cup water (if required)

2 Tbsp fish sauce

1 tsp sugar

salt to taste

handful fresh basil leaves (optional)

- Since this curry cooks very quickly, start by cooking the rice (see page 44).
- Heat the oil in a frypan or wok. Stir in the curry paste and cook for about a minute, then add the onion, potato and lime leaves (if you can find them). Stir-fry for 1–2 minutes.
- Add the chicken and stir, then carefully pour in the coconut cream and simmer for 5 minutes, stirring occasionally.
- Add the vegetables and bamboo shoots (if using) and thin sauce with ¼–½ cup water if required. Simmer until chicken is cooked through and vegetables are just tender, about 10 minutes in all, then add the fish sauce and sugar. Taste and add salt if required, then stir in the basil leaves (if using).
- Serve over rice garnished with a few extra basil leaves.

BUTTER CHICKEN

Stir-fried Chicken with Vegetables

Once you get used to stir-frying chicken and vegetables, you will find it is very quick. The marinade flavours and glazes the chicken, and the vegetables become brightly coloured and tender-crisp. Get out everything you need and prepare the ingredients before you start cooking, so nothing is overcooked.

For 2 servings

cooked rice (see below)

200–300g boneless chicken breasts or
    thighs
1–2 tsp grated root ginger
1 large clove of garlic, thinly sliced
1 Tbsp light soy sauce or Kikkoman soy
    sauce
1 Tbsp sherry
1 tsp brown sugar
1 tsp instant chicken stock or ½ tsp salt
2 tsp cornflour
3–4 cups of prepared vegetables (see
    step two of method)
4 tsp canola or other flavourless oil
1 Tbsp water

- Cut the chicken into thin slices (5mm thick) across the grain of the muscle. Cut long strips into shorter pieces. Put the chicken in a plastic bag with the next seven ingredients, knead the bag lightly to mix everything, then leave to stand for at least 15 minutes.
- Select and wash four or five of the following quick-cooking vegetables, with a variety of colours and textures. Have the prepared vegetables about the same size as the chicken. Use broccoli or cauliflower florets, sliced thinly; tender, inner celery stalks sliced diagonally; button mushroom slices; small zucchini, sliced crossways; red, yellow or orange capsicums, cut in thin strips; baby spinach leaves or 2-cm wide slices of larger spinach leaves; or spring onion leaves, sliced diagonally. (If preparing these before they are needed, put in a large plastic bag, and refrigerate until required.)
- Seven minutes before you want to eat, put a large frying pan over high heat, swirl half the oil round the hot pan, then tip all the prepared vegetables into the pan and cook them quickly, stirring constantly and tossing with a heat-proof stirrer. Add the water, cover the pan and cook 1–2 minutes longer, until they are tender crisp, then tip everything into a bowl.
- Heat the pan on high heat again, add the remaining oil, then the chicken and its marinade. Stir-fry for a minute or two, until the chicken has lost its raw look and is cooked. Add the vegetables from the bowl, stir them through the chicken and serve immediately on the cooked rice.

Rice:

Before starting to stir-fry, put ¾ cup of long-grain rice in a microwave dish with 1½ cups of boiling water and ¼ tsp salt. Cover lightly and microwave at 70% for 12–15 minutes, then leave to stand for 5 minutes before serving.

Easy Fruity Chicken Casserole

This is an easy mixture to make because it does not need to be browned. Use dark soy sauce to give the casserole a good colour, and use onion soup for extra flavour and to thicken the sauce.

For 6 servings

12 chicken thighs
1½ cups apple and orange juice
1½ tsp dark soy sauce
2 cloves garlic, chopped
1 packet onion soup mix

- Heat the oven to 180°C with a rack just below the middle.
- If possible, choose a casserole or baking dish which will hold the chicken pieces in one layer. Coat the baking dish with non-stick spray.
- Mix the juice, soy sauce, chopped garlic and onion soup mix in the casserole or baking dish, then add the chicken pieces, with their best side down.
- Put on a lid or cover with foil, pressing down the edges, then bake for 1 hour. If possible shake the casserole or pan occasionally to make sure the chicken does not stick.
- Take off the lid or cover and turn the chicken pieces over carefully. If the liquid seems too thick, add about half a cup of water to thin it down. Cook uncovered for about 15 minutes longer, adding extra water if the sauce is too thick.
- Serve on rice, pasta or mashed potatoes, with broccoli or another green vegetable.

Smoked Chicken Coleslaw

This useful and substantial salad can be served for lunch or the main part of an evening meal, with crusty bread alongside, at any time of year, but it always seems especially good in spring. Try it just like this, then make your own variations — we do!

For 3–4 servings

Dressing

2 Tbsp canola or other flavourless oil

2 tsp sesame oil

2 Tbsp fish sauce or Kikkoman soy
  sauce

2 Tbsp fresh lime or lemon juice

1 Tbsp sugar

a few drops of hot chilli sauce

350–400g boneless smoked chicken
  meat

Coleslaw

600–700g (½ a fairly large) cabbage,
  shredded thinly

1 small or medium red onion

1 large carrot

1–2 cups very thinly sliced celery stalks

¾–1 cup roasted peanuts

- Make the dressing by mixing the first six ingredients together. Taste and add a little extra sugar and some salt, if you think it necessary. Set aside while you prepare the salad.
- Cut the smoked chicken into several strips lengthways, then cut the strips crossways into small pieces, and put aside.
- Cut away the core of the cabbage, shred the remaining cabbage very thinly, crossways, and put it in a large bag or bowl. Halve the red onion from top to bottom, cut it crossways into very thin slices and mix the pieces evenly through the cabbage. Cut the carrot diagonally into long, thin shreds and add to the cabbage mixture, then add the sliced celery and mix everything together.
- Chop the roasted peanuts on a board, using a large, sharp knife.
- Refrigerate the dressing, chicken, vegetables and peanuts in separate, covered containers for several hours, or serve immediately.
- Just before serving, combine everything in a large bowl and mix gently but thoroughly, preferably with your fingers, so the chicken, vegetables and nuts are lightly coated with dressing, then pile up the salads in separate shallow bowls.

. . . .

Chicken Fried Rice

This one-pan meal is an 'anglicised' version of a Chinese recipe. It is quick to make if you have cooked rice and cooked chicken to hand. It does, however, take only a little longer to start with raw chicken — just skin thighs or breasts, cut them into small pieces and cook in a small amount of butter or oil in the large pan you will use for everything else, then put the chicken pieces aside.

For 3–4 servings

4 tsp instant chicken stock

1 Tbsp Kikkoman soy sauce

1 Tbsp sugar

½ cup water

2–3 Tbsp canola oil

1–2 cloves garlic, finely chopped

1 fairly large onion, chopped

1 cup sliced brown button mushrooms

1 red pepper, chopped

1 cup sliced celery, optional

2 cups sliced cabbage

1–2 cups cooked chicken meat

2–3 cups of cooked, long-grain rice

sliced spring onion leaves

- Have everything prepared before you start cooking, as the final result will not be good if you overcook the food at any stage. Vegetables should be chopped in pieces about 5mm thick and no longer than 2–3cm. Mix together the instant chicken stock, soy sauce, sugar and water in a small container.
- Heat a large pan, preferably with a non-stick finish. Add 2 Tbsp of the oil, then the chopped garlic and onion. Toss over high heat for about 30 seconds, then add the remaining vegetables and the extra oil. Toss well to coat lightly with oil, then cover the pan and cook for 3–4 minutes, until the vegetables are tender-crisp, without letting them brown.
- Add the cooked chicken and the mixed liquid, stirring it through the vegetables, then the cold, cooked rice. Keep turning and stirring the mixture until everything is hot.
- Serve straight away in shallow bowls, garnished with thin, diagonally sliced spring onion leaves if available.

Beef

VISITORS OFTEN COMMENT ON THE QUALITY OF CATTLE GRAZING PEACEFULLY ON LUSH PADDOCKS, FROM ONE END OF THE COUNTRY TO THE OTHER. TRY THESE POPULAR BEEF RECIPES AND SEE FOR YOURSELF JUST HOW GOOD OUR BEEF TASTES.

PAN-GRILLED STEAK

Pan-grilled Steak

Many New Zealanders enjoy a tender, juicy, nicely cooked steak!

- Fillet steak is the most tender and most expensive steak. Other fairly tender steaks such as sirloin, rib eye or rump steaks, although they cost less than fillet per kilo, are considerably larger, so you may find that the price of a smaller, very tender fillet steak is little more than the price of a larger, not-so-tender steak. Think twice, too, before you choose any steak which has been sliced thinly. Although each steak will cost less, it is hard to cook a thin steak so it browns outside but remains juicy and pink inside.
- Organise yourself before you cook steak, so that you have the accompanying foods ready at the same time. The vegetables you are serving with your meal should be almost cooked and ready to serve.
- We like to cook steak in a (preferably fairly heavy) dry frying pan, which has been preheated so it is very hot before the steak is put in.
- A minute or so before cooking the fillet steak, turn in a well-flavoured mixture of soy sauce, Worcestershire sauce, a few drops of oil and crushed garlic, so both sides are very lightly coated.
- Place the steaks in the very hot pan. (Closely packed steaks make steam and don't brown well.) Don't keep turning them. It is best to turn a steak only once, after the first side has browned evenly.
- When the steak has cooked to the stage you like it — this depends a little on the thickness of the steak, try 2 minutes per side for rare, 3 minutes per side for medium rare or 4 minutes per side for medium — put it aside on a warmed plate in a warm, but not hot, oven for 3 or 4 minutes. The steak will become more tender as it stands.
- If you like a dribble of pan juices poured over the steak, add a little stock, wine or vegetable liquid to the now-empty pan and swirl it round. Add a small knob of butter and swirl the liquid round again until you are left with 1–2 tsp of well-flavoured buttery liquid to drizzle over the steak just before serving.

Barbecued Steak

When the evenings are warm and still, it is very pleasant to sit and relax around the barbecue, waiting for meat (and perhaps some vegetables) to be cooked and served with a salad and eaten outside.

- If you are cooking fillet steak on a solid plate, follow the instructions above, putting the flavoured steak on a clean, pre-heated plate. Since the steak has a little oil on it, it is not necessary to oil the hot plate.
- If you plan to cook the steak on a rack, make sure the rack has been thoroughly cleaned. For best results, we rub the heated rack with a little oil on a paper towel, just before the steaks are laid on them. Don't move the steaks around as they cook, and turn them only once. If you can, leave the steaks to stand for 5 minutes or so before eating them.

30-minute Bolognese

Our version of this classic sauce has probably strayed a long way from the original Italian version, but it is still very good, and always well received.

For 4–6 servings
2 Tbsp olive oil
1 medium onion, diced
2 cloves garlic, chopped
1 medium carrot, finely diced
1 stick celery, thinly sliced
400–500g lean minced beef
½ tsp dried basil
½ tsp dried marjoram
400g can whole or diced tomatoes
300g can tomato purée
½–1 tsp salt
black pepper to taste
400–500g long pasta (e.g. spaghetti)
½ Tbsp olive oil or butter

- Heat the oil in a large pan. Add the onion and garlic and cook for 2–3 minutes, stirring frequently, until the onion is soft.
- Stir in the carrot and celery and cook for a minute longer, then add the beef. Cook, stirring frequently until the beef has lost its pink colour. Add the herbs, tomatoes and tomato purée. Season to taste wth salt and pepper.
- Allow the mixture to boil, then reduce the heat to a gentle simmer and cover with a lid. Simmer gently for 10–15 minutes, stirring occasionally, while you cook the pasta (if the sauce begins to look dry, add a ¼ cup pasta water or wine).
- Drain the cooked pasta and toss it with the oil or butter, then arrange on individual plates or a platter. Spoon the sauce over the pasta and top with chopped parsley and/or grated Parmesan. Serve accompanied by a salad or vegetables and crusty bread.

HOME-MADE HAMBURGERS

Home-made Hamburgers

It's hard to beat a good, home-made hamburger. Hot off your own stove or barbecue, they really are quite different from anything you can buy. Not only are they quick and easy to prepare, but they taste great and are popular with children.

For 4 'quarter-pound' burgers
500g minced beef
1 cup (2–3 slices bread) soft
   breadcrumbs
1 large egg
1 tsp garlic salt
black pepper to taste

- Place all the ingredients in a large bowl, then mix thoroughly (clean, wet hands work best for this). Divide the mixture into 4 balls and flatten into roundish patties.
- Grill or barbecue about 20cm from the heat, turning when browned. Alternatively, brown on both sides in a hot, lightly oiled frypan, lower heat and cook until the centre is firm when pressed.
- Serve in lightly toasted plain or sesame buns with three or four of the following: sliced **tomato**, torn or shredded **lettuce** (or coleslaw), sliced **cheese**, fried **egg**, red, yellow and green **capsicums** (raw or roasted), sautéed **mushrooms**, sliced **gherkins** or **dill pickles**, thinly sliced **red onion**, crisped by soaking in cold water, sliced **avocado**, sliced **beetroot**, **watercress** or other fresh **herbs**, **chilli beans** and **sour cream**. Of course, no burger is complete without **tomato sauce** and/or **mustard**.

Easy Spaghetti & Meatballs

Baking meatballs instead of browning them in a pan saves time and effort — you can cook the pasta and make the sauce while the meatballs are in the oven.

For 4 servings
2–3 thick slices or end crusts of bread
1 small onion
1 clove garlic, peeled
500g lean minced beef
1 egg
1 tsp ground fennel seed (optional)
½ tsp each dried basil, oregano,
   thyme and chilli powder
1 tsp salt
400g fresh or dried spaghetti

Sauce
1 Tbsp olive oil
2 cloves garlic, peeled and chopped
2 x 400g cans whole tomatoes in juice
½ tsp each dried basil and oregano
½ tsp salt
black pepper to taste
½ cup red or white wine
1–2 Tbsp butter
grated Parmesan and/or chopped
   basil or parsley to serve

- Heat the oven to 220°C. Break the bread into smaller pieces and chop finely in a food processor. Add the onion (cut in about 8 pieces) and garlic, and chop finely. Add the next 7 (8 if using fennel seed) ingredients and mix in bursts, just until everything is combined. (Over-mixing toughens the meatballs.) Divide mixture in quarters, then each quarter into 8 balls, rolling them with wet hands.
- Arrange the meatballs in a single layer in an uncovered baking pan lined with Teflon or baking paper and bake for 12–15 minutes, or until a halved meatball is no longer pink in the middle.
- While meatballs bake, cook the spaghetti in plenty of lightly salted boiling water, and prepare the sauce.
- Heat the oil in a large pan and cook the garlic for about 1 minute. Add tomatoes (with the juice) to the pan, forcing the solids through a large sieve with the back of a spoon (discard the seeds and any tough bits that remain). Add the seasonings and wine, and allow the sauce to simmer and reduce down for about 5 minutes. The sauce doesn't need to be too thick, just thick enough to coat the meatballs.
- Drain the cooked pasta, return it to the cooking pot, and toss it with 1–2 Tbsp butter, then divide between plates. Either add the meatballs to the pan with the sauce, toss to coat and spoon over the pasta, or spoon the sauce over the pasta, then top with the meatballs. A sprinkling of grated Parmesan and/or chopped parsley or basil makes a nice finishing touch.

Chilli con Carne

We think Mexican food is great! The staples required (tortillas, bottled chillies, canned beans etc) no longer need to be hunted out at specialist stores and can generally be found in their own little niche on supermarket shelves — a sure sign of popularity.

This basic beef and bean mixture can be used in a number of different ways — it's good served over rice, or makes a great filling for tacos and burritos, and can also be used for nachos.

For about 4 servings
1 Tbsp canola or other oil
1 large onion, preferably red
2 cloves garlic, peeled and chopped
½–1 tsp minced chilli or chilli powder
350–500g minced beef
2 tsp ground cumin
1 tsp each oregano, salt and sugar
400g can kidney beans
2 Tbsp tomato paste
about ½ cup water

- Heat the oil in a fairly large non-stick pan. Add the finely chopped onion, the garlic and chilli, and cook on moderate heat for 1–2 minutes. Raise the heat and add the minced beef, breaking it up and browning it.
- Stir in the cumin, oregano, salt and sugar, the beans and their liquid, the tomato paste and water, and cover and simmer for about 10 minutes. Add extra liquid if mixture is too thick to spread easily, or cook uncovered if it seems very liquidy.

Tacos, Tostadas, Burritos & Nachos

Taco shells are corn tortillas that are fried or baked until crisp and folded over into a U-shape. A tostada is simply a tortilla (usually corn), cooked in the same way, but left flat. Instead of being filled, like tacos, tostadas simply have the same fillings piled on top. To serve tacos or tostadas, either give everyone their own shells and have them help themselves from bowls of fillings, or assemble them yourself before serving.

Fillings
Chilli con Carne (above)
grated cheese
very finely shredded lettuce
finely grated carrot

Optional extras
chopped olives
diced tomatoes
diced capsicums (or chillis)
sliced avocado (or guacamole, see
   page 10)
sour cream
chilli sauce or salsa
chopped fresh coriander
sliced spring onions

NOTE: *The fillings above are in the order we like to add them, i.e. start with the mince mixture, then add cheese, then lettuce etc, finishing with guacamole, sour cream and/or chilli sauce.*

Be warned, there is no easy and/or neat way to eat tacos and tostadas — use your fingers and accept that a little mess is part of the fun!

Burritos
A burrito is a soft flour tortilla wrapped around your selected fillings. Soft flour tortillas can be bought in various sizes of about 20–40cm in diameter.

- Fillings for burritos are exactly the same as for tacos and tostadas. However, if you are using the extra large tortillas you may want to add a little rice. To fill a burrito, lay on a flat surface. Arrange the fillings in a line that runs about ½ of the way from top to bottom (don't be too generous with the fillings or your burrito will be difficult to roll and almost impossible to eat!)
- When you have finished adding fillings, fold the bottom up over the filling, then fold one edge in, followed by the other so the whole thing resembles a tall skinny envelope. Again, these can be assembled in the kitchen or at the table. (Wrapping the burrito in a napkin will make it easier to eat.)

Nachos
In their simplest form nachos are just corn chips with melted cheese over them, but by adding Chilli con Carne and a few other optional extras, you can turn them into a substantial meal.

corn chips (any flavour)
grated cheese
Chilli con Carne (see above)
selected optional extras (as for tacos)

- Preheat the grill while you place a pile of the heated mince mixture in the centre of a flat (ovenproof) plate or platter. Pile the corn chips around this, then sprinkle them liberally with your selected extra toppings and grated cheese. Grill until the cheese has melted. Top with a dollop of sour cream and/or guacamole and a splash of chilli sauce or salsa. Serve immediately.

CHILLI CON CARNE

LAZY LASAGNE

Roast Lamb

Roast lamb is a traditional all-time favourite with many Kiwis. Here are two versions you may like to try.

Roast Leg of Lamb with Vegetables & Gravy

- Heat oven to 170°C with a rack just below the centre. Cut off and discard any excess fat from the leg of lamb.
- Rub the lamb with a mixture of Kikkoman soy sauce and lemon juice, if you like. If you have any fresh rosemary, pierce the meat with a sharp knife, six to 10 times, and push a mini-sprig of rosemary into each cut, OR put slivers of garlic in slits cut in the lamb.
- Stand the lamb, meaty side up, in a roasting pan and roast uncovered for 1½–2½ hours, depending on its size and your preference. For accuracy use a meat thermometer, pushing it deeply into the lamb (the tip must not touch bone).
  - Rare (pink) lamb: 65°C (150°F)
  - Medium lamb: 70°C (160°F)
  - Well-done lamb: 80°C (175°F)
- Remove from the oven, cover with foil and leave it to stand in a warm place for 15–20 minutes before carving it in slices, across the grain of the meat.

- To roast vegetables around the lamb (suitable vegetables are potatoes, kumara, pumpkin, parsnips, onions, etc), scrub or peel them, cut into even-sized pieces, dry and put them in a large plastic bag. Add 2–4 Tbsp oil, close the bag, and move the vegetables round in it until they are lightly coated with the oil. Place around the lamb 1¼ hours before you expect the meat to be cooked.
- To make gravy, lift the cooked meat and vegetables from the pan and keep them warm. Pour off accumulated fat, leaving about 2 Tbsp. Put the pan over medium heat and stir 2–3 Tbsp of flour into the remaining oil. Keep stirring until the flour is light brown, then add about 2 cups of vegetable cooking liquid, or stock made by mixing 1 tsp of instant stock into 2 cups of water. Stir over moderate heat until the liquid thickens, season to taste and pour into a jug.

Stuffing for Roast Lamb

- A lamb leg, forequarter or shoulder which has had the bones removed (usually by a butcher, although you can do it yourself) is good stuffed. If you buy a boneless leg or shoulder, which is encased in a stretchy net, you can remove the net, open the lamb flat, and put home-made stuffing inside it. Roll up again, skin-side out. (If preferred, ask a butcher to bone a leg or shoulder of lamb for you.) Position your stuffing on the lamb so you can roll the lamb around it, covering it completely. Tie the lamb around the stuffing with loops of string, or sew it up neatly, using a darning needle and light string or heavy thread.

- Roast as above. (Be careful to not push a thermometer into stuffed lamb with its tip touching stuffing rather than lamb, as you will get an inaccurate reading.)
- To make stuffing, cook a chopped onion in 2 Tbsp butter until it is transparent, then take it off the heat and add a little salt and pepper. Add chopped parsley or other herbs if you like, then stir in the finely grated rind of an orange, a lightly beaten egg and 2 cups of breadcrumbs made by crumbling or food-processing stale bread. Half a cup of finely chopped dried apricots is a nice addition, too.

Mint Sauce

We're not actually big mint sauce fans, but from the responses we had there are clearly some people who feel roast lamb and mint sauce go together like hand and glove!

For about ½cup

1 bunch/punnet mint (about 10g)
1 Tbsp sugar
¼ cup boiling water
¼ cup wine vinegar
salt to taste

- Strip the leaves from any tough stalks, then chop the mint finely (a little food processor does this well). Put the mint in a small bowl or jug (or leave in the processor) and add the sugar.
- Pour in the boiling water, stir until the sugar dissolves, then add the vinegar. Leave to cool to room temperature, then season to taste with salt.
- Transfer to a small jug and serve, with roast lamb of course!

Lamb Shanks with Macaroni

We think that this is perfect comfort food for the end of a cold day, when things haven't gone as well as they might have. Know the feeling? These shanks will make you feel that the world is a better place!

For 4 large or 8 smaller servings

8 lamb or hogget shanks

3 medium-sized onions, quartered

4 cloves garlic, chopped

1 x 170g (about 160ml) jar tomato
　　paste

4 cups boiling water

1–2 tsp dried oregano

1 Tbsp Worcestershire sauce

1 Tbsp sugar

1½ tsp salt

3–4 sprigs rosemary

1 cup macaroni or other small pasta
　　shapes

- Heat the oven to 170°C with a rack just below the middle. Rub the shanks with a little oil, if you like, then put in a large roasting pan with the quartered onions and the chopped garlic. Spray the onions and garlic lightly with a little cooking spray, or brush lightly with a little oil, and put in the oven so the onions can brown a little.
- Mix the next six ingredients in a large jug and pour the mixture over the meat. Lie the rosemary sprigs between the shanks, then cover the pan tightly with a lid or with two strips of foil, which have been folded together to join them, and folded tightly over the edges of the pan.
- Bake for 1½–2 hours, until the meat is tender, then lift off the lid or foil, remove the rosemary and add the pasta, making sure it is all under the surface of the liquid. Cover again and cook for 30 minutes longer or until the pasta is tender.
- Lift out the shanks and gently mix the pasta, sauce and onions together, adding a little water or vegetable cooking liquid if it needs thinning. Serve in shallow bowls, rather than flat plates, with a green vegetable such as cabbage, broccoli or Brussels sprouts.

Lamb's Liver & Bacon

When it is briefly cooked, lamb's liver is tender, moist and delicious, as well as most nutritious. Because it cooks very quickly, anything that you plan to serve with it should be cooked first.

For 4 servings

4 rashers bacon

2 tsp butter or canola oil

300–400g lamb's liver

¼ cup flour

½ tsp garlic salt

½ tsp freshly ground pepper

½ tsp freshly ground nutmeg, optional

Gravy

flour

butter or oil

½ cup apple juice or water

1–2 tsp Worcestershire sauce

- Cut the bacon rashers in half if they are long, and snip the rind to stop them curling up as they cook. Heat oil or butter in a fairly large frypan and cook bacon at moderate heat for about 3–4 minutes or until crisp. Keep warm.
- Using a sharp knife, cut the liver into slices about 5mm thick. Keep the knife slanted, so the slices are wider and more attractive. Trim away and discard any fibrous or unattractive pieces.
- Mix the flour and next three ingredients together. Working quickly, dip both sides of each piece of liver in the seasoned flour then put in the hot bacon fat in the pan. Cook several pieces at a time. Turn each slice as soon as it has cooked (about 30 seconds). Take each piece from the pan when you can pierce it in the middle and see no pink juice. Cook the rest of the liver in batches, adding a little butter or oil to the pan if necessary.
- If you like gravy with liver and bacon, put about 2 tsp of the leftover dipping flour mixture in a little extra butter or oil in the pan and stir until it browns lightly, then stir in the apple juice or water. Add a little Worcestershire sauce, taste and adjust seasonings, and spoon a little of this gravy over each serving.

Liver & Bacon Kebabs

These make a great lunch or light evening meal for lovers of lamb's fry.

- Cut lamb's liver into 2cm cubes. Sprinkle the cubes with finely chopped fresh sage leaves and lemon juice. Cut strips of thinly sliced streaky bacon into 12–15cm lengths, and spread each strip with a little Dijon mustard. Roll each strip (mustard side inside) round a cube of liver, then thread the rolls on shortish skewers, three or four rolls per skewer. Cook these under a grill, on a barbecue rack, or in a hot pan containing a film of oil, until the bacon is crisp on both sides. Serve immediately with fresh crusty bread and a salad.

LAMB SHANKS WITH MACARONI

LAMB KEBABS

Lamb Kebabs

Pita pockets stuffed with this tasty marinated lamb and salad make a great, easy meal. The skewered lamb cubes can be cooked either under the grill or on the barbecue. We like to use pita breads that are about 12–15cm across, splitting and stuffing them, but you can use larger ones of course. Just roll them round the filling rather than stuffing it into the pocket.

For 4–6 servings
1 medium onion
4 cloves garlic
4 Tbsp olive oil
2 tsp cumin
2 tsp thyme
1 tsp oregano
½ tsp chilli powder
½–1 tsp ground black pepper
400–600g lean cubed lamb

To serve
½ cup natural yoghurt
2 Tbsp lemon or lime juice
½ tsp paprika
about 2–3 cups shredded lettuce
about ¼ cup thinly sliced red onion
couscous tabouleh (see below)
4–6 pita breads

- Measure the first eight ingredients into a food processor or blender and process to form a smooth paste. Place the lamb in a bowl (or plastic bag), then add the marinade paste and stir until the meat is well covered. Leave to stand for at least 20 minutes, or preferably longer. (For a really good flavour, the marinade and lamb can be mixed the night before and refrigerated until required.)
- Thread the marinated lamb onto skewers and arrange on a foil-covered baking sheet. Place 5–10cm from a hot grill and cook (or place directly on a pre-heated barbecue) for about 5–7 minutes, turning occasionally until the outside begins to blacken slightly but the inside remains a little pink. Allow the cooked meat to stand for about 5 minutes before serving.
- While the lamb cooks, prepare the sauce by combining the yoghurt, lemon or lime juice and the paprika. Prepare the lettuce and onion and tabouleh.
- To serve: Brush the pita breads with a little water or oil if they feel dry, then warm them by microwaving for 15–20 seconds each. Halve and split the pita breads (if desired). Fill each with a little shredded lettuce, some tabouleh, a few slices of onion and 6–8 cubes of lamb. Add a spoonful or two of the sauce and serve. (There is no tidy way to eat these — fingers work best so provide plenty of napkins or paper towels.)

Lamb Cutlets with Couscous Tabouleh

This is a good meal for a hot summer evening. When you buy cutlets, make sure that they are 'chined' with the knobbly bit at the top of the rib bone removed.

For 2–3 servings
6–9 (chined) lamb cutlets

Marinade
1 tsp chopped or minced garlic
2 tsp lemon juice or 1 tsp balsamic
    vinegar
¼ tsp crumbled dried oregano
1½ Tbsp olive oil

Couscous Tabouleh
¾ cup couscous
½ tsp salt
½ tsp minced chilli
1¼ cups boiling water
2 Tbsp lemon juice
2 spring onions
2 cups cubed red tomatoes
about ¼ cup chopped mint
¼–½ cup chopped parsley
2 Tbsp olive oil

- Put the chops between two sheets of plastic (or a large folded plastic bag) and beat with a rolling pin until the eye of the meat is twice its original size.
- Stir the marinade ingredients together on a large shallow plate and turn the cutlets in the mixture. Cover with plastic and leave to stand while you prepare the tabouleh. Heat a large non-stick frypan.
- Put the couscous, salt and chilli in a medium-sized bowl. Stir in the boiling water and lemon juice and leave to stand, without stirring, for about 6 minutes. Meantime, finely slice the spring onions, including most of the leaves. Cut the tomatoes into 1cm cubes and finely chop the mint and parsley.
- Put the cutlets in the pan and cook about 1½ minutes per side.
- While lamb cooks, fork the spring onions, tomatoes, herbs and olive oil through the tabouleh and pile on plates. Serve cutlets or kebabs leaning against the tabouleh as soon as lamb is cooked. Serve alone or with crusty bread.

Tapenade-rubbed Butterflied Lamb

As we mentioned earlier, lamb is a great Kiwi favourite, but probably doesn't often get used on the barbecue as anything other than chops. A butterflied (boned then spread out flat) shoulder or leg of lamb cooks really well, and surprisingly quickly, on the barbecue — it's great if you're looking for something a little special.

Tapenade is a paste made from olives, anchovies and capers. It is sometimes served with bread or crostini as a dip or spread, but in this case we use it as a rub (rather like a very thick marinade) to flavour the lamb before barbecuing. Olives and anchovies may not be everyone's favourites, but despite their strong flavours, they don't dominate this dish — they just add a delicious savoury flavour.

For 6–8 servings
1.2–1.5kg butterflied shoulder or leg of lamb*
about ¼ cup tapenade (see the recipe below or use pre-prepared)
about 1 Tbsp olive oil

*If you can't find a butterflied leg/ shoulder in the chiller, ask the butcher to prepare one for you — they'll usually do it while you wait.

- Place the lamb skin-side up on a board and lightly score through the fat in a diamond pattern. Rub half the tapenade over this side of the meat, then turn it over and rub the remaining tapenade into the other side.
- Place the meat in a large shallow dish, cover with cling film and leave to stand for at least 15–20 minutes (refrigerate overnight if desired).
- Preheat the (preferably hooded) barbecue. Drizzle the lamb with the olive oil, then place it on the grill side of the barbecue and cook it over a high heat for 5 minutes per side (uncovered), then transfer it to the hotplate side and cook (covered if possible) over a medium–high heat for a further 10–12 minutes per side. (If using a meat thermometer, inserted at the thickest part it should read about 60–63°C when the lamb is cooked). Rest the lamb for 10 minutes before carving.
- Serve with crusty bread and Greek Summer Salad (see page 18). Enjoy!

Tapenade

This makes more than you need for the recipe above, but the extra keeps well in the fridge and can be used as a dip for vegetables or a spread for bread or crostini.

For about ½ cup
1 clove garlic, peeled
125–150g pitted black olives
3–4 Tbsp lightly packed fresh parsley
3–4 anchovy fillets, plus a little of their oil
1 Tbsp capers
1 Tbsp olive oil
1 Tbsp lemon juice
freshly ground black pepper

- Place the garlic, olives and parsley in a food processor and process until well chopped. Add the anchovy fillets, plus 2–3 tsp of the oil they were packed in, and the capers. Process again until well mixed. Pour in the olive oil and lemon juice and process to make a smoothish paste (how smooth is up to you). Season with a little freshly ground black pepper.
- Use immediately with the shoulder of lamb or transfer to a clean airtight container and store in the fridge for 1–2 weeks. Serve with crackers or crostini and a selection of chopped fresh vegetables for dipping.

Pork

ROAST PORK AND HAM USED TO BE
OCCASIONAL TREATS, BUT TIMES CHANGE,
PRICES DROP, AND PORK DISHES ARE NOW
POPULAR ALL YEAR ROUND.

STUFFED ROAST PORK WITH CRACKLING

Stuffed Roast Pork with Crackling

Kiwis really enjoy roast pork, especially when it is served with crunchy, crisp, golden crackling. If you haven't prepared this before, we suggest that you talk to your friendly butcher and tell him what you are looking for. Our favourite is a boneless loin of pork, wide enough to roll up with stuffing inside, weighing 1½–2kg. If the skin is still on it can be cooked in place, but if it's already removed, cook the skin separately as crackling.

For 8–12 servings

Stuffing

about 8 prunes
about 8 dried apricots
1 orange
about 8 spinach leaves
3 slices bread
1 egg
½ tsp salt
½ cup chopped parsley

1.5–2kg boneless loin of pork
1–2 Tbsp each soy sauce and mustard
1 Tbsp oil
½–1 tsp salt

- First prepare the stuffing. Halve the prunes and chop each dried apricot into 5 or 6 pieces. Grate the rind from the orange and put it aside, then simmer the chopped apricots in the juice squeezed from the orange until it has been soaked up. Cook the spinach leaves in a little boiling water until they soften and are bright green, then drain. Crumble the bread, preferably in a food processor, then mix in the egg, orange rind, salt and chopped parsley.

- If the skin is still attached, lie the pork skin side up on a board. Using a sharp knife (a handyman's utility knife with snap-off disposable blades is ideal), cut long thin strips through the skin, but not right through the fat underneath it. Make a few crossways cuts too, so the cooked crackling can be broken into manageable lengths after cooking.

- Lie the pork skin-side down and brush the inside with a mixture of soy sauce, mustard, oil and salt, then spread the bread mixture evenly over it, starting at the side closest to the centre of the pig's back, leaving 2–3cm uncovered along the opposite side. Arrange the prunes and apricot mixture in rows on the stuffing, nearest the centre back, then squeeze the spinach dry and arrange it in a line parallel to the fruit. Have several lengths of string ready and roll up the pork, starting from the centre back and finishing with the uncovered edge. Tie the lengths of string neatly round the rolled meat.

- If the skin was removed, brush the outside of the meat with a little more of the soy sauce mixture and sprinkle with flour. If the skin is still attached, rub lightly with oil, and sprinkle the surface thinly but evenly with salt. Rub it into the cuts so the surface is fairly smooth. Put the prepared roll of pork in a roasting pan, with the join down, and bake at 180°C for about 1½ hours, or until a meat thermometer registers about 74°C (or 165°F).

- If you are cooking the skin separately, score it as described above and place in a shallow tray. Rub lightly with oil, then sprinkle the surface thinly but evenly with salt, rubbing it into the cuts so the surface is fairly smooth. Put it into the oven, skin-side up, soon after the roast is put in. Take it out when the surface is nicely blistered, crisp, and golden brown, probably after an hour or so.

Gravy

- Pour most of the fat from either pan after the roast pork or crackling is removed. Stir 3 Tbsp flour into the remaining drippings and let it brown lightly, then stir in about 3 cups altogether of vegetable cooking liquid and apple or orange juice and season to taste.

Marmalade-glazed Baked Ham

A ham always looks more festive if you glaze and decorate the outer surface before you slice and serve it.

- Peel or cut the skin from a cooked ham. You can remove it all or leave the skin around the shank intact, so you can move the ham from one place to another, holding on to skin rather than a fatty surface. It is usual to cut down through the skin with a narrow-bladed, sharp knife, making a zigzag edge rather than a straight cut around the shank. (Each side of the Vs that you cut should be 5 or 6cm long.)
- Start cutting and lifting away the skin from the side of the ham that rests on the plate. It is usually easiest to pull off the skin with only a little of the fat underneath attached. After you have lifted off all the skin you want removed, you can cut off as much of the fat layer as you like, using a sharp knife. The remaining fat is then usually scored in diamond shapes. (Do not cut through the flesh under the fat as you do this.)
- Make your glaze by heating about a cup of your favourite marmalade with 2–3 Tbsp of orange juice until it bubbles vigorously. Strain through a sieve to remove all the strips of skin, then brush the glaze all over the exposed surface of the ham.
- You can push a clove through the fat and flesh where the diamond cuts intersect, or you can push toothpicks, each holding a piece of pineapple topped with a red crystallised cherry (or just one of these) into the ham, in the centre of each diamond shape. Brush the pineapple and cherries with glaze too.
- It looks particularly attractive if you then brown the marmalade glaze. You can do this by placing it low down under a hot grill, in a hot oven, or with a kitchen blow torch. Take care not to burn the glaze, whichever method you use. NEVER leave the ham unattended while it is browning.
- As you carve the ham, lift out the cherry, pineapple and toothpicks from the part being cut, and serve with the ham.

Sweet & Sour Pork

Kiwis have something of a soft spot for sweet and sour mixtures — so here's our version! We prefer to stir-fry (rather than deep-fry) the pork as it seems more tender, is simpler, and obviously lower in fat. Like any stir-fried dish, it pays to prepare and measure everything before you start cooking, as once you begin, everything happens very quickly.

For 4 servings

450–500g pork fillet
3 Tbsp Kikkoman soy sauce
2 cloves garlic, peeled and chopped
2 tsp grated ginger
1 small to medium-sized onion
1 medium-sized carrot
1 medium-sized red or green pepper
  (or half of each)
¼ cup tomato sauce
3 Tbsp brown sugar
1 Tbsp wine vinegar
1 Tbsp cornflour
½ cup cold water
2 Tbsp canola or other oil
salt and pepper to taste

- Halve the pork fillet/s lengthways, then cut these crossways into slices about 7mm thick. Place the sliced pork in a plastic bag and add the soy sauce, garlic and ginger. Massage the bag so everything is mixed and the marinade covers the meat. Leave to stand for 10–15 minutes (or refrigerate overnight).
- Halve and peel the onion, then cut it lengthways onto thin (5mm) strips. Peel the carrot and cut it into sticks about 5mm square and 5cm long, then halve and core the pepper/s and cut these into thin strips too.
- Measure the tomato sauce, brown sugar and vinegar into one small bowl, then combine the cornflour and water in another.
- Heat 1 Tbsp of the oil over a medium-high heat in a large, preferably non-stick, frypan. Add the marinated pork and stir-fry for 3–5 minutes until the pork is lightly browned (it doesn't have to be cooked through at this stage). Transfer the pork to a bowl and set aside.
- Add the remaining oil to the pan, and when hot, add the sliced onion. Stir-fry for about a minute, then add the carrot, cook for another minute, then add the pepper strips. Stir-fry for about a minute longer, then add the pork (plus any juices) and the tomato sauce and cornflour mixtures. Cook, stirring frequently for 3–4 minutes longer, until the sauce has thickened and the pork is cooked through.
- Season to taste with salt and pepper, then serve over steamed rice.

Bacon & Egg Pie

Alison's mother, Margaret Dickie, was brought up on a North Canterbury sheep station. The family of nine (plus farm hands) gathered round the big table for meals — all produced on the coal range — three times a day! As a result, Margaret and her three sisters all learnt to be good cooks. After she married, Margaret cooked lovingly and enthusiastically for her husband, three 'hollow-legged' daughters, and later for her grandchildren! With children helping — and learning — she made Bacon and Egg Pies several times a week, and these were enjoyed at home, taken on picnics, added to school lunches, and given to neighbours. Many years later, Alison and Simon still make the same pies.

For 8 servings

Quick Flaky Pastry (see page 77)

4–6 rashers of lightly cooked bacon, chopped

about 1 cup cooked peas

1–2 cups chopped cooked potatoes or kumara

5 large eggs

- Heat the oven to 200°C with a rack in the middle, then make the pastry.
- Prepare the pastry according to the recipe on page 77. Roll this out on a floured board to make two rounds, each 30cm across.
- Ease one lot of pastry into a 23cm pie plate. Spread half the chopped bacon, peas and potato or kumara into it. Put the eggs in the bowl in which the pastry was mixed, and beat with a fork until the yolks are broken and the eggs look streaky. Pour about half the eggs over the mixture in the crust, then add the remaining bacon, peas and potatoes, etc, and dribble the rest of the egg over the top.
- Moisten the edge of the pastry in the plate, then place the other pastry sheet on top of the filling, trimming the edges if necessary. Crimp the edges if you like. Make a hole in the centre, decorate the pie with shapes made from the pastry trimmings and brush the top with milk.
- Bake at 200°C for about 40 minutes. Serve warm, reheated or cold.

VARIATION: *Use 2 squares of bought pastry instead of home-made pastry, rolling it out more thinly, if necessary. Replace the bacon with 2–3 ham steaks, cubed.*

Tex-Mex Ribs

Pork ribs smothered in this 'Tex-Mex' barbecue sauce are so good! Including chocolate in the sauce may sound unusual but it is used in some Mexican dishes and the combination works well.

For 3–4 servings

2 Tbsp canola or olive oil

1 medium onion, peeled and finely chopped

2 cloves garlic, crushed, peeled and chopped

½ tsp chilli powder

½ tsp ground allspice

1 cup water

6 Tbsp tomato paste

¼ cup balsamic vinegar

25g (5 squares) dark cooking chocolate

1.5–2kg meaty pork ribs

- Heat the oven to 180°C.
- Heat the oil in a medium pan. Add the onion and garlic and cook, stirring frequently, until the onion is soft. Stir in the chilli powder and allspice and cook for about a minute, then stir in the water, tomato paste and balsamic vinegar. Allow the mixture to boil, then remove from the heat. Break up the squares of chocolate and add to the mixture, stirring occasionally until the chocolate has melted and is evenly mixed in.
- Cut the ribs between the bones so they are in 2–3 rib sections (this makes them more manageable to eat). Thoroughly non-stick spray or line a large roasting pan with a Teflon liner or baking paper. Spread the ribs over the bottom in a single layer, then pour in the sauce. Turn the ribs several times so they are coated with the sauce.
- Place the pan in the middle of the oven and cook for 50–60 minutes, turning the ribs and basting with the sauce after 30 minutes.
- Serve with rice or potato wedges (see page 72) or mashed potatoes, and a green salad or coleslaw.

BACON & EGG PIE

Vegetable Sides

WHETHER YOU GROW THEM IN YOUR BACKYARD, CHOOSE THEM AT A FARMERS'MARKET, OR SELECT THEM FROM THE COLOURFUL PRODUCE SECTION AT YOUR SUPERMARKET, VEGETABLES ARE SO INVITING THAT YOU CAN'T PASS THEM BY.

CITRUS-BAKED KUMARA

Citrus-baked Kumara

Kiwis clearly identify kumara as one of their favourite vegetables. Their lovely sweetness is particularly good when combined with a hint of citrus, as it is in this recipe.

For 6 servings

4 medium kumara (about 1kg)
50g butter
grated rind of 1 lemon and 1 orange
¼ cup brown sugar
½ tsp grated nutmeg
½ cup orange juice

- Cook the scrubbed, unpeeled kumara in a covered container in a microwave or conventional oven until just tender. Stand until cool enough to work with, then cut into slices about 1cm thick, removing the skins if you want to. Arrange the slices in a large, flat ovenware dish which has been non-stick sprayed or lightly buttered.
- Warm butter until melted. Add remaining ingredients and heat until the sugar dissolves, then pour the mixture over the kumara. Bake at 180°C for 30 minutes, or until the surface is crisp and golden brown. Serve immediately.

VARIATION: *If serving as part of a vegetarian meal, add coarsely chopped roasted peanuts and/or sunflower seeds.*

'Twice-baked' Potatoes

These are a great way to use up all sorts of odds and ends, and are always very popular. Small amounts of ham and/or salami, or salmon, tuna, baked beans, spaghetti, etc can easily be incorporated into the same basic mixture. Depending on the filling/s used, they can then be served as the main part of a meal or as an interesting side dish.

For 3–4 servings

3–4 medium-sized (about 150g each)
 all-purpose or floury potatoes
25g butter
¼–½ cup sour cream or milk
½–1 cup extra 'bits' (chopped ham,
 salami, sliced cooked sausages or
 other diced cooked meats, salmon,
 tuna, spaghetti, baked beans,
 chopped cooked vegetables, etc)
1–1½ cups grated cheese
¼–½ tsp salt
pepper to taste

- Scrub the potatoes, poke a few holes in each with a fork or skewer, then microwave on High (100%) power until just cooked, probably about 6–8 minutes. Turn them once after about 4 minutes. Leave to stand until cool enough to handle.
- Heat the oven to 180°C. Halve the potatoes lengthways and scoop out most of the insides into a bowl, leaving a 'shell' about 7mm thick. Warm the scooped-out potato in the microwave if completely cold, add the butter, sour cream or milk and mash thoroughly. Stir in your selected filling/s, about two-thirds of the cheese and season to taste with salt and pepper.
- Spoon the mashed mixture back into the 'shells', arrange on a baking paper or foil-lined oven tray and sprinkle each with a little of the remaining cheese.
- Bake for 15–20 minutes, then remove from the oven and leave to stand for about 5 minutes before serving.

EASY RATATOUILLE

Easy Ratatouille

We love this late-summer/early-autumn dish, and it's nice to know we're not alone! This shortcut version, which takes 45 minutes, makes a large quantity that can be served over two meals.

For 6–8 servings

¼ cup olive oil

2 medium-sized eggplants

4 red, orange and yellow peppers

4 green and/or yellow zucchini

4 large onions

1½ tsp (2 cloves) minced garlic

up to ¼ cup extra olive oil

2 x 400g cans whole tomatoes

2 tsp sugar

1 tsp salt

2 Tbsp basil pesto

2–3 Tbsp chopped fresh herbs

- Make this in the largest, heaviest (lidded) pot, frying pan or flame-proof casserole dish that you have. Heat the first measure of olive oil and add the unpeeled eggplant, sliced peppers and zucchini, all cut in 2cm chunky pieces. Cook over a medium to high heat for 15 minutes so that the vegetables brown lightly but do not steam in large amounts of watery juices. Add the onions (chopped into similar-sized pieces), the garlic, and enough extra oil to stop the mixture sticking or burning. Raise the heat slightly, and cook for 15 minutes longer, until the onions are transparent and lightly browned. (Cook the vegetables in batches if you find this easier.)
- Stir in the tomatoes (and juice), add the sugar, salt, pesto and herbs, and bring to the boil with the lid ajar.
- Cook on medium heat so the liquid bubbles and thickens, but the vegetables do not burn. We like the stew at the stage where the liquid is quite thick but the vegetables still have some firmness, after about 15 minutes of simmering. Taste and adjust seasoning.
- Serve in bowls, with chunks of firm, crusty bread as a complete meal OR serve on pasta or rice, topped with parmesan cheese OR ladle generous amounts into a pot of cooked, drained, firm potatoes, heat through, and serve in bowls.

VARIATION: *To reduce cooking time, use less oil and maximise flavour, brush the thickly sliced eggplant with olive oil and brown in a contact grill (on medium setting). Repeat with the halved peppers and zucchini and thickly sliced onions. When browned, cut in cubes and simmer with the remaining ingredients, as above.*

Vegetables à la Grecque

These vegetables are delicious served warm or at room temperature with barbecues or grilled meat. They have a rather chewy texture and the sauce around them, flavoured with coriander seeds, is very good sopped up with a bread roll.

For 3–4 servings

600g prepared vegetables

2 cloves garlic, chopped

2 Tbsp olive oil

2 Tbsp wine vinegar

1 tsp coriander seeds, crushed

½ tsp sugar

½ tsp salt

425g can Mexican or Italian-flavoured tomatoes

¼ cup chopped parsley

1 Tbsp lemon juice

- Cut one or several types of vegetables into long strips. Use carrots, runner, French or yellow beans, cauliflower, celery, green or yellow zucchini, scallopini, mushrooms, or yellow, orange, red or green capsicums.
- Cook the chopped garlic in the oil without browning. Stir in the vinegar, crushed coriander seeds, seasonings and tomatoes, then add the vegetables, cover and simmer for 10–15 minutes or until tender-crisp, turning vegetables at intervals.
- Sprinkle with parsley and lemon juice and serve the vegetables warm or cold, but preferably at room temperature, in their sauce in a shallow dish.

Wedges

Wedges make an ideal accompaniment for all sorts of dishes and are a great snack, or even a light meal, on their own.

- Heat the oven to 220°C. Quarter potatoes lengthways (allow 1–1½ medium potatoes per person), then cut each quarter (lengthways) into 3 wedges. Place wedges in a plastic bag and toss with 1–2 tsp oil per potato. Arrange wedges in a single layer on a non-stick-sprayed or Teflon or baking paper-lined tray. Sprinkle lightly with garlic salt, paprika and pepper then bake for 12–15 minutes or until golden brown.
- Perfect to serve alongside fried fish, burgers or steaks, or with sour cream and tomato sauce on their own.

Mashed Potatoes

Mashed potatoes are comfort food with a capital C! A pile of light, fluffy, creamy mashed potatoes can be the highlight of a meal, whether you are cooking for yourself, your family or guests. It's worth taking a little time and trouble over their preparation, so they finish up absolutely perfect. Start with main crop floury potatoes — new or waxy potatoes will not turn out to be fluffy.

Stovetop Mashed Potatoes

- Wash or scrub the potatoes you are going to cook. Cut them into even-sized pieces.
- Bring a pot of lightly salted water to the boil. Drop in all the potatoes and check that the water covers them. Cover with a lid so the potatoes are surrounded by water or steam.
- Drain the potatoes when they are tender right through when pierced with a knife. Pour off the cooking liquid and save it for later use in a gravy or sauce. If you have time, allow the drained potatoes to stand in the dry pot for 2–3 minutes.
- Mash with a potato masher or push the potatoes through a potato ricer. Add 1 tsp of butter per serving. Lastly, beat the mashed potatoes with a fork, adding milk and some of the cooking liquid until they are light, smooth and creamy. Season as needed.
- Serve immediately or leave to stand in a warm place for a few minutes before serving.

Microwaved Mashed Potatoes

It is hard to give accurate timing for cooking potatoes in a microwave because of the difference in cooking time between potato varieties and the varying levels of power in microwave ovens. Keep a note of how long it takes to cook a certain weight of potatoes, especially if you buy in bulk. After a little experimenting and accurate timing, you should be able to produce consistently good results.

- Cut peeled floury or all-purpose potatoes into 1–2cm cubes.
- Add 1 tsp butter and 1 Tbsp water per serving.
- Cover and cook on High (100%) for 2–3 minutes per serving, shaking to reposition the potato cubes about halfway through the cooking time.
- Leave to stand for 5 minutes after cooking, then test to make sure all the cubes are cooked through completely.
- Mash without draining, adding milk, salt and pepper to taste. Then beat with a fork until they are light, smooth and creamy.

NOTE: *Should the microwaved potato cubes appear to be slightly shrunken when you check them after cooking, you have cooked them too long. Next time you cook the same variety, allow half a minute less per serving.*

Scalloped Potatoes

Although we often use the microwave to make scalloped potatoes for two, we tend to cook a family-sized dish in the oven, usually alongside a meat loaf or similar. If you aren't in the habit of making scalloped potatoes, do try this recipe — we think it will win you over.

For 4 servings

600g medium all-purpose or floury
    potatoes
2 Tbsp (25g) butter
1–2 cloves garlic or 2 small onions,
    finely chopped
1 tsp salt
pepper to taste
1 cup milk

- Heat the oven to 200–220°C, positioning the rack just above the centre. (Set the temperature to 220°C if you plan to cook something else at the same time; 200°C if the potatoes will be on their own.)
- Choose even-shaped potatoes that will look more attractive when layered. Thinly peel or scrub them with a pot scourer. Cut the potatoes into thin, crossways slices and put them in a bowl of cold water.
- Lightly coat the inside of a shallow ovenware dish with non-stick spray.
- Heat the butter in a small pot, but don't let it brown. Add the garlic or onions, stirring until heated through. Add the salt, pepper and milk.
- While the milk heats, drain the potatoes and arrange them in the prepared dish. Flatten them with your hand or with a fish slice, then evenly pour over the hot milk mixture.
- Cover with a lid, a sheet of foil or baking paper folded over loosely at the edges, and bake for 20–30 minutes. Uncover and bake for a further 15–30 minutes until the top is golden brown and the potatoes feel tender when pierced with a sharp knife.
- Serve with a meat loaf, chops or sausages, etc, and vegetables.

NOTE: *Use a large shallow dish, rather than a smaller, deeper one so you get a nicely browned layer on the surface.*

Oakhill Potatoes

A 'Potato Bake' was another slightly ambiguous dish that kept cropping up on our subjects' lists. This dish, that Alison has often made over the years, is one that Simon ranks very near the top of his list of 'ultimate comfort foods', so it's hopefully the sort of thing people meant. We know we love it anyway . . .

For 4–6 servings

4 large (about 800g) cooked
    all-purpose or floury potatoes
2 hard-boiled eggs, peeled and
    roughly chopped
2 rashers bacon
1 medium onion
50g butter
¼ cup flour
1 tsp dry mustard
1 tsp salt
2 cups milk
¼ cup grated tasty cheddar cheese
1 Tbsp butter
1 cup fresh breadcrumbs

- Slice the cooked potatoes into a shallow, sprayed or buttered baking dish. Add the eggs. Chop the bacon and onion and cook them together in the first measure of butter in a large pot until the onion is transparent. Stir in the flour, mustard and salt, half the milk, and bring to the boil, stirring constantly. Add the remaining milk and bring to the boil again. Take off the heat and stir in the grated cheese straight away. If the sauce seems too thick to pour easily, thin it with extra milk. Pour the sauce over the potatoes, covering the entire surface.
- Top the sauce with buttered crumbs made by melting the second measure of butter and stirring it into the crumbs.
- Refrigerate for up to 24 hours or bake immediately, in the middle of the oven, at 180°C for 30–45 minutes until the potato mixture has heated through and the crumb topping is golden brown.
- Serve as part of a buffet dinner or as a family meal with a salad and small bread rolls.

VARIATION: *For a vegetarian meal, leave out the bacon and use twice as much cheese.*

Desserts

MANY A KIWI HAS A SWEET TOOTH, AND REMEMBERS THE FAVOURITE DESSERTS OF THEIR CHILDHOOD. ALTHOUGH DESSERTS ARE OFTEN NOW AN OCCASIONAL TREAT, THERE WASN'T A SINGLE PERSON WHO DIDN'T LIST THEIR FAVOURITE. THE BIG SURPRISE FOR US WAS THAT LEMON MERINGUE PIE (JUST) PIPPED PAVLOVA FOR THE TOP SPOT!

LEMON MERINGUE PIE

Lemon Meringue Pie

Lemon Meringue Pie never goes out of fashion. Alison's mother used to make it for Sunday dinner dessert when Alison was a student, and Peter, now her husband of 40-plus years, biked from the other side of the city, then climbed a steep hill, to visit! Who knows — if this, his favourite dessert, had not been on the menu regularly, he might have stopped coming!

For a 20cm pie

1 cup flour
70g cold butter
about ½ cup cold water

Filling

1 cup sugar
rind and juice of 2 lemons
½ cup cornflour or custard powder
1½ cups water
2 Tbsp butter
3 large egg yolks

Meringue

whites of 3 large eggs
pinch of salt
½ cup castor sugar

- Heat the oven to 220°C, then make and cook the pastry shell. Mix the flour and cubed, cold butter in a food processor. While processing in short bursts, add about half the water. Add the remainder a few drops at a time, until the crumbs come together to form a ball of dough, then stop mixing immediately. Roll out the dough and shape it over an upturned, 20cm diameter, metal pie plate. Trim, dampen and fold back the edges and prick the shell all over, so it will not puff up as it bakes (still upside down) for 10–12 minutes or until golden brown. Take out the shell, cool, then lift it carefully off the tin and stand it, right way up, in a bigger pie plate.
- To make the filling, process the sugar and the lemon rind (cut the rind off the lemons with a floating blade peeler) in the unwashed food processor. Add the cornflour or custard powder and the water. Process to mix, then transfer the mixture to a microwave-proof bowl. Microwave on High (100%), stirring every 1 or 2 minutes, until it is clear and evenly thick. Stir in the butter and egg yolks, heat again, just until the filling bubbles and thickens, then stir in the lemon juice. Do not heat again. Pour the hot filling into the shell.
- Using a beater, beat the egg whites and salt until they form peaks that turn over at the tips, then add the castor sugar and beat again to the same stage. Pile the meringue onto the filling in spoonfuls, then swirl the meringue attractively on top, making sure the meringue touches the shell at the edges.
- Bake at 190°C until the tips are lightly browned. Do not overcook at this stage. Leave the pie to stand at room temperature. Serve in slices, cutting the pie with a sharp knife with a wet blade.

Tamarillo & Apple Crumble

There is something that seems almost magical about tamarillos. Maybe it's the colour, or the smooth skin or just the seemingly perfect symmetry of the fruit, but more likely it's the combination of all three. If you aren't actually quite sure what to do with them, try this revamped version of an old family favourite.

For 4–6 servings

4 ripe tamarillos
4–6 Tbsp brown sugar
3 medium Braeburn or Granny Smith
    apples
1 tsp cinnamon
½ cup quick cooking rolled oats
½ cup shredded coconut
½ cup sliced almonds
½ cup plain flour
½ cup brown sugar
1 tsp cinnamon
½ tsp mixed spice
100g cold butter, cubed

- Heat oven to 180°C. Cut an x at the bottom of each tamarillo, place in a small bowl and cover with boiling water, leave to stand for about a minute, then drain and slip off the skins.
- Cut the flesh into wedges, place in a larger bowl, then add the brown sugar and toss (you can do this up to a day in advance if you like). Peel and slice the apples and add them to the tamarillos with the first measure of cinnamon.
- Non-stick spray a 20 x 30cm casserole dish and spread the fruit mixture over the bottom. (OR dsivide between individual ovenproof bowls or ramekins.)
- Measure the remaining ingredients into a food processor (fitted with the chopping blade), and process until well mixed and crumbly looking. Sprinkle the topping evenly over the fruit, then place in the oven and bake for 35–40 minutes until golden brown.
- Serve with ice cream, softly whipped cream or creamy yoghurt.

Instant Strawberry Ice Cream

This delicious ice cream takes only ONE minute to make! You can make it right through the year if, during the strawberry season, you freeze chopped strawberries in packets, each containing 2 cups of chopped berries. The recipe will not work if you do not start with free-flow, hard, completely frozen strawberries that have been cut in fingertip-sized pieces.

For 4 servings
2 cups frozen (diced) free-flow
    strawberries
½ cup icing sugar
about ½ cup chilled cream

- Get out the ingredients and measure the icing sugar before you start.
- Break up the strawberries if they are in a frozen block. Chop large berries or pieces of berries into 5–10mm cubes. (The fruit MUST be frozen hard, free-flow and in fairly small pieces when it is used.)
- Tip the frozen, free-flow berries into the food processor bowl. Work quickly so the fruit stays very cold. Process with the metal chopping blade until fruit is finely chopped and has turned into 'strawberry dust' (usually in 10–20 seconds). This is a noisy operation! Without delay, add the icing sugar and process briefly until mixed.
- With the machine running, add a thin stream of the chilled cream through the feed-tube, until a smooth, frozen cream has formed. The amount needed varies from batch to batch. Stop as soon as the mixture is evenly textured and creamy.
- This ice cream is best served immediately, but it may be put in a covered container in the freezer and used within a few days if you like.

Trifle

We don't think there's anyone in New Zealand who doesn't know what a trifle is — and who doesn't remember their own mother's trifles with nostalgia! Although your mother's trifle was probably served in a large, cut-glass bowl, we prefer to make individual ones in glasses because they look so pretty.

Choose several of the following
sheet sponge
sherry and/or concentrated fruit juice
raspberry or strawberry jam, optional
passionfruit pulp or passionfruit
    topping, optional
canned peaches or ripe mango or
    other fruit
fresh raspberries and/or strawberries
strawberry or raspberry jelly (the cold
    water variety)
vanilla custard, home-made or bought
lightly whipped sweetened cream or
    plain Greek yoghurt

- Use suitable glasses, made of glass or clear plastic, which hold about 1 cup. We usually choose straight-sided, clear, good-quality plastic glasses because they are easy to layer the food in and easy to eat from, although stemmed, straight-sided glasses and stemmed wine glasses look attractive.
- Choose several foods from the list at left. After you have made a trifle once or twice, you will know how much of each you need. (Leftover ingredients can be used in different ways, so nothing is wasted.)
- A small packet of sheet (unfilled) sponge goes a long way. Cut a round shape from a piece of sponge using the glass in which you will put the trifle, pushing it down right at the edge of the block of sponge. Cut the round in half to make 2 rounds. This is as much sponge as you need for 1 serving. If preferred, break pieces of sponge into pieces and place in the glass for the bottom layer. (Wrap and freeze unused sponge for later use.)
- Spoon 1–2 Tbsp of a mixture of sherry, juice (from canned peaches) or concentrated fruit juice, and some jam if you like, over the piece of sponge in the bottom of the glass. Add passionfruit pulp if you like.
- Next, add a layer of fruit. It looks pretty if you use peaches or mango etc, and put some red berries in this layer. Keep the pieces of fruit fairly small and position them close to the edge of the glass. Add a few spoonfuls of red, set jelly if you are using it. Follow with a few spoonfuls of custard, then some whipped cream or yoghurt. It looks prettier if the various layers are not flattened.
- Repeat the layers, finishing with whipped cream and a small piece of fruit.
- Refrigerate until serving.

Crème Brûlée

Crème Brûlée seems to be something of a new favourite with Kiwis! It is an unashamedly rich dessert and we think it is best served in fairly small quantities. If you don't like the idea of using cream only, you can use a mixture of equal parts cream and milk but, interestingly, the full-cream version sets a little firmer than the milk and cream version, so in some ways the latter can actually seem creamier in the mouth.

For 4–6 servings

2 cups cream (or cream and milk mix, as above)

2 vanilla pods (optional)

4 large egg yolks

½ cup sugar

1 tsp vanilla essence

⅛ tsp (pinch) salt

4–8 tsp caster sugar

- Pour the cream (or milk and cream) into a small pot or microwave bowl. Add the vanilla pods (if using) and heat gently until it just boils.
- Place the egg yolks, first measure of sugar, vanilla essence and salt in another bowl and whisk together. Remove the vanilla pods (if used) then pour the hot cream mixture into the bowl and whisk again. (If you did use the vanilla pods, you can split them lengthways, gently scrape out the tiny black seeds and add these to the mixture too.)
- Pour the mixture through a sieve to remove any lumps, then carefully pour the mixture into the ramekins (small dishes), leaving a few millimetres at the top of each. Arrange the ramekins in a sponge roll tin or roasting pan and carefully pour in enough hot water to fill to about halfway up the outsides of the ramekins.
- Place the tin or pan in a preheated oven and bake at 150°C for 25–30 minutes or until the custard has just set (it will still appear a little jiggly, but not runny), then remove from the oven.
- Brûlées are quite versatile and can be served while still quite warm in cool weather, or in warmer weather (or if you're working in advance) cool to room temperature or even refrigerate until required. Just before serving, sprinkle the top of each ramekin evenly with 1–2 tsp of caster sugar (use the smaller quantity for small ramekins or more for larger ones).
- Arrange the ramekins on a tray and place under a very hot grill (3–5cm from the heat) for 2–3 minutes until the sugar melts and browns. (You can do this with a blowtorch.) Remove from the heat and let the caramelised sugar cool and harden to form a crisp layer. Serve immediately.

Pastry

Quick Flaky Pastry

For 1 thinly rolled double crust 20–23cm pie

1¼ cups flour

1 tsp baking powder

125g cold butter

about ½ cup milk

1 tsp wine vinegar

- Mix the flour and baking powder. Grate butter or cut it into about 25 small cubes, and rub or cut into the flour, by hand or with a food processor. (Pieces of butter should be visible when pastry is rolled out.) Mix the milk and vinegar, and add this gradually to flour mixture until it is just moist enough to form a fairly stiff dough. Divide the dough in two, then roll out thinly.

Sweet Short Pastry

100g butter

½ cup sugar

1 egg

1 cup plain flour

1 cup self-raising flour

- Soften but do not melt the butter; add the sugar and egg then beat until well combined. Stir in the unsifted flours and mix well to form a dough. If too dry, add a little (teaspoon by teaspoon) milk. If too soft to work with, refrigerate rather than adding more flour.
- Roll the pastry out on a lightly floured board before trimming to a round 3–4cm larger than the tin to be used. (Note: This will make more pastry than is required for a single tart. The extra can be frozen or refrigerated for later use).

APPLE PIE

Apple Pie

Apple Pie is right up there in terms of comfort foods! Even starting from scratch and making your own pastry, it really is very easy and the enthusiasm with which it will be greeted (and the smell of the pie baking) is definitely worth the small amount of effort required.

For a 20–23cm pie

1 recipe Quick Flaky Pastry (see page 77)
½ cup sugar
2 Tbsp flour
4–6 apples
25g butter, melted
6 cloves or ¼ tsp ground cloves (optional)

- Make the pastry according to the recipe, then cut it in half. Roll each piece out thinly and evenly on a lightly floured board, turning often. You should have two rounds a little bigger than a 20 or 23cm pie plate. Put one piece in the plate, with its edges overhanging, stretching it as little as possible.
- Put the sugar and flour in a bowl. Coarsely shred or slice the peeled or unpeeled apples, and toss them in the sugar and flour. Pour the melted butter over the apple, add the cloves if you like them, and toss to mix.
- Put the prepared apple into the pastry-lined plate, dampen the surface of the remaining pastry, and place on the apple, dampened side down. Press the two layers of pastry together, trim about 1cm beyond the edge of the pie plate, then fold the overhanging pastry under, pinching the layers together. Flute or fork the edges if desired, make one central hole or several holes for steam to escape. Brush with lightly beaten egg if you want a glazed surface. Bake at 220°C until golden brown and the apple is tender when tested with a skewer, lowering the heat to 180°C if the pastry browns before the apple is cooked.
- Serve warm, with cream, ice cream, yoghurt or fromage frais.

Upside-down Apple Pie (Tart Tartin)

This Upside-down Apple Pie is one of our all-time favourites! Although it may take a little practice to get it just right, it is well worth the trouble.

For 6–8 servings

50g butter
½ cup sugar
about 1kg small (kiddy-size) tangy apples
½ tsp each powdered cloves and cinnamon (optional)
1 sheet pre-rolled flaky or short pastry

- Heat oven to 200°C with a rack in the middle. Use a cast iron frypan about 25cm across, if possible, or use a pan AND a pie plate of about the same size. Melt the butter in the pan, then sprinkle the sugar over it and leave to melt on moderate heat. Tilt the pan as the sugar caramelises, but do not stir it, or let it darken too much.
- Peel, core and halve the apples. Leave them to stand in lightly salted water until you have prepared them all. (If you use large apples, cut them in quarters.) Place the apples outer-side down in the pan. Cover them loosely and push them closer together as they soften. Turn the apples a few times, so the other sides soften and brown a little, too. After about 10 minutes, the apples should be soft enough to lie close to each other, and their outer sides should be amber. Arrange the apples so the rounded sides are down in the cast iron pan, or arrange them similarly in the pie plate, with all the syrup from the pan. Sprinkle the apples with the spices if you like.
- Roll out the sheet of pastry so you have a circle as big as the frypan (or pie plate). Lie the pastry on the warm apples, then push the edges down between the pan (pie plate) and the apples, so the edge of the pastry is close to the base of the pan/pie plate. Pierce the pastry top in a few places, then bake until the pastry is evenly golden brown, about 15 minutes.
- Place a flat plate on top of the pan/pie plate, then quickly turn everything over so the pan/pie plate is upside down and the tart is on the plate, pastry-side down. Lift off the pan/pie plate, and rearrange the apples, if necessary. Serve the warm pie in slices, topped with lightly whipped cream or vanilla ice cream.

Pavlova

That Pavlova should score so highly on a list of favourite New Zealand desserts was hardly a surprise! Everybody's grandmother probably had her own secret recipe, but here's our favourite version. It's a simplified version where everything goes into the mixer at once, but still works very well. (This isn't an enormous mixture, but you can double it if you want.)

For 1 large pavlova
1 cup caster sugar
2 tsp cornflour
¼ tsp salt
1 tsp wine vinegar
½ tsp vanilla
½ cup (3–4) egg whites

NOTE: *Because ovens vary, cooking times may need slight changes. Pavlovas with space below the crust and compacted middles have been cooked too long. If centres are not completely set, cook a little longer next time. Fan bake for the first 10 minutes if you have this option. If fan baking for whole time, lower temperature by about 10°C.*

- Using standard, level cups and spoons for everything, measure the caster sugar, cornflour and salt into a clean, dry bowl. (Any traces of fat in the bowl or on the beater will stop eggs beating up.) Stir together.
- Add the vinegar and vanilla, then measure and add the egg whites, taking care to get absolutely no yolk in the mixture. Beat with an electric mixer at high speed for about 15 minutes until a thick, non-gritty meringue forms. When you lift out the mixer blades, the peaks should stand up stiffly, or just bend over at their tips.
- Cover a baking sheet with baking paper, then pile the mixture onto this into a round shape about 25cm across.
- Bake in a preheated oven at 100°C for 60 minutes, then turn off oven and leave for 30 minutes longer. Take out of oven after this time.
- Leave unwrapped, in a cool place, up to 2 days. To serve, top with whipped cream. Decorate traditionally with strawberries, kiwifruit or passionfruit or use other fruit. Drizzle chocolate topping over strawberries if desired.

VARIATION: *Use double quantities for a large Pavlova. Pile on baking paper or bake in a paper-lined round 20 or 23cm tin. Bake for 1¼ hours and leave in oven for 15 minutes longer.*

Bread & Butter Pudding *with Rum Sauce*

Even though you may have childhood memories of stodgy and rather boring bread and butter puddings, you should try this one — it's actually quite light and the combination of the rum sauce with the warm-custardy bread is wonderful!

For 4–6 servings
50g stale white bread or stale bread rolls
3 eggs
1½ cups milk
½ cup cream
3 Tbsp brown sugar
1 tsp vanilla essence
apricot jam to glaze

- Heat the oven to 180°C.
- Cut the bread or bread rolls into slices and lay them in an oval or rectangular buttered baking dish that holds 4–5 cups of liquid. (Give the dish a good coating with non-stick spray first — it will make cleaning up much easier.)
- Break 2 of the eggs into a bowl, then separate the last one, adding the white to the bowl with the other eggs and reserving the yolk for use in the sauce. Mix the milk, cream, sugar and vanilla into the eggs.
- Pour the custard mixture over the bread and leave to stand for 10 minutes. While the bread soaks, place a roasting pan containing 2–3cm of hot water in the oven. Place the baking dish in the water bath, then bake, at 180°C for 30–45 minutes, until the custard under the bread is set in the middle.
- Lift the dish out of the roasting pan. Gently brush surface with warmed apricot jam to glaze, and serve warm, with Rum Sauce (below).

Rum Sauce

50g butter, melted
¾ cup icing sugar
3–4 Tbsp rum

- To make the Rum Sauce, melt the butter in a bowl over boiling water, then stir in the reserved egg yolk and the icing sugar. When this mixture is very hot and has thickened a little, lift the bowl away from the heat, allow to cool for a few minutes, then stir in the rum.

PAVLOVA

Dee's Cheesecake

This is our favourite cheesecake. Smooth, rich and creamy, it is very hard to resist, and we find that refrigerated, leftover cheesecake has a habit of disappearing at any time — day or night!

For 8–12 servings
1 packet (250g) digestive biscuits
100g butter
3 x 250g cartons cream cheese
1 cup sugar
1 tsp vanilla
2 large or 3 medium eggs
berries, icing sugar or passionfruit
    topping, to serve

- Heat the oven to 160°C with a rack a little below the middle.
- Crumb the biscuits in a food processor or put them in a plastic bag and crush them with a rolling pin. Melt the butter until it is just liquid, and stir in the biscuit crumbs. Press the mixture over the bottom and up the sides of a 20 or 23cm loose-bottomed, round cake pan, using the back of a spoon.
- Beat the cream cheese and sugar until soft and fluffy, using a food processor or beater. Beat in the vanilla then the eggs, one at a time, then pour the mixture carefully into the biscuit-lined pan.
- Bake for 40–50 minutes until the centre is firm, without letting the top brown. (Cover the top of the pan with a piece of baking paper if it looks as if it is starting to brown.) Turn off the oven and leave the cheesecake in it to cool.
- Refrigerate when cold, for up to 4 days. Just before serving, either top with berries or other fruit and sprinkle with icing sugar, or cover with passionfruit topping, or serve the berries alongside each wedge, or spoon a little passionfruit topping over each cut slice. (Dip a knife in hot water just before cutting each slice, for smooth cut edges.)

Steamed Carrot Pudding

Puddings like this definitely come into the category of comfort food! What could be better than the spicy smell, moist texture, and rich colour of a steamed carrot pudding at the end of a cold, blustery winter's day!

For 4–6 servings
100g butter, barely melted
2 cups (200g) grated carrot
1 large egg
1 cup brown sugar
1 cup plain flour
½ tsp baking soda
1 tsp each cinnamon
    and mixed spice

NOTE: *To steam this pudding, choose a bowl of at least 5-cup capacity, checking that it is heatproof and will fit inside a large pot with a tight-fitting lid. Stand the bowl in the pot on a folded cloth, pot-scrub or crumpled foil to keep it off the bottom. We use a metal or Pyrex bowl, and cover the pudding with foil, pressing the foil at least 5cm down the sides.*

- Heat the butter until it is almost liquid. Grate the carrots. (We use the food processor, tip them out, then replace the grating plate with the mixing blade and put the grated carrots back in the food processor.) Add the warmed butter, egg and brown sugar, process or mix briefly, then add the flour, baking soda and spices. Process/stir until just mixed. If the mixture is too dry to tip from the bowl, add enough milk to get it to a dropping consistency. If the mixture is too liquid, add a little extra flour. (This depends on the moistness of the grated carrot.)
- Coat the bowl in which the pudding will be steamed with a little softened butter or with non-stick spray. Spoon the mixture into the bowl. Level off the top and cover the bowl with foil, firmly pressing it about 5cm down the sides. Lower the bowl into a pot (prepared as suggested at left), with enough warm water to come half way up the sides. If it is a tight fit, make a sling to lower and lift it out easily later. (A string bag works well!) Put on the pot lid.
- Bring the water round the pudding to the boil, then simmer gently for 2–2½ hours, checking occasionally to make sure the pot does not boil dry. Turn the pudding out onto a flat plate a few minutes after it has been taken out of the pot.
- If you make the pudding ahead you can unmould it, cover it with cling film and reheat it in a microwave at a Low power level. You can also cut and wrap a few slices when they are needed, and warm them in a microwave just before serving them.

DEE'S CHEESECAKE

STICKY DATE PUDDINGS

Sticky Date Puddings

There is something particularly nice about being served your own little pudding for dessert, so instead of baking one big pudding, we usually bake these in muffin tins.

For 6 individual (or one 23cm square) pudding/s

1 cup (about 175g) pitted dates, chopped
1 cup hot water
50g butter
1 cup self-raising flour
½ tsp baking soda
1 tsp cinnamon
½ tsp mixed spice
¾ cup lightly packed brown sugar
2 large (size 7) eggs

- Place the roughly chopped dates in a medium-sized microwave bowl. Cover with the water and microwave on High power (100%) for 5 minutes, stirring occasionally. Stir in the butter, then set aside to cool.
- Sift the flour, baking soda and spices into another medium-sized bowl, and stir in the brown sugar. Add the eggs to the date mixture, stir until well combined, then fold this into the dry ingredients.
- Divide the mixture between six large non-stick sprayed or oiled muffin pans, or pour it into a prepared 23cm square cake tin. Cover muffin tins with foil, then place in a roasting pan containing 2cm of boiling water. Bake at 180°C (or 170°C fan-bake) for 25–30 minutes, until puddings are firm when pressed in the centres. Leave to stand for 5 minutes before removing from pans. (Bake the large pudding uncovered for 30 minutes or until centre is firm when pressed.)
- Serve warm topped with Butterscotch Sauce.

NOTE: *Each large muffin tin holds about 1 cup of mixture. Use other containers if preferred.*

Butterscotch Sauce

¾ cup sour cream
¾ cup brown sugar
2 Tbsp orange liqueur
   or grated rind of ½ an orange

- Combine all ingredients and heat until sugar dissolves. (For a thicker sauce, simmer, stirring frequently, for 5–10 minutes.)

Self-saucing Chocolate Pudding

We make several different versions of this incredibly popular pudding, depending on how we intend to cook it. Obviously it works well in a slow cooker, but it can also be baked in the oven if you prefer.

For 6 servings

1 cup self-raising flour
½ cup sugar
¼ cup cocoa powder
¼ tsp salt
½ cup milk
¼ cup canola oil
1 Tbsp vanilla essence
½ cup chocolate chips

Sauce

¾ cup sugar
¼ cup cocoa powder
1½ cups boiling water

- Heat the oven to 180°C and non-stick spray a 1.5–2 litre casserole dish.
- Sift the flour, sugar, cocoa powder and salt into a large bowl. In a small bowl whisk the milk, oil and vanilla together. Pour into the dry ingredients, then fold everything together gently until just combined. Sprinkle in the chocolate chips and stir just enough to incorporate them. Pour or spoon the pudding batter into the slow cooker insert or casserole dish.
- Make the sauce by combining the sugar and cocoa powder with the boiling water. Stir or whisk to ensure there are no lumps, then carefully pour over the batter, getting as much as possible around the edges rather than all in the middle.
- Place the uncovered casserole dish in the oven and bake at 180°C for 30–35 minutes or until the centre feels about as firm as the edges.

Baking

KIWI COOKS ARE OFTEN RENOWNED FOR
A BAKED ITEM WHICH THEY CAN PRODUCE
AT THE DROP OF A HAT! THESE KIWI
FAVOURITES ARE NOT DIFFICULT OR TIME
CONSUMING, BUT WE ARE SURE THEY WILL
ALL BE POPULAR.

LOLLY CAKE

Lolly Cake

We were surprised to see the number of Kiwis who put 'Lolly Cake' on their list of favourite foods. We have asked bakeries if it sells well, and have been told that it always quickly disappears from their shelves. When Alison made her first-ever batch and gave little packets to her friends, they all told her how much they had enjoyed it, so now we know for sure that it is not just a children's treat!

For 24 squares
125g butter
½ can sweetened condensed milk
  (about 200g)
1 tsp vanilla
250g packet malt biscuits
180–250g 'Eskimos' or 'fruit puffs'
coconut to coat

- Melt the butter for 1 minute on High (100%) in a large microwave-proof bowl big enough to hold all the ingredients. Stir in half a tin of condensed milk (this is about 200g) and the vanilla. Mix well, warming the mixture for about 30 seconds on High if it does not mix smoothly.
- Crumb the malt biscuits, half the packet at a time, in a food processor, using the metal chopping blade, and tip the fine crumbs into the bowl. (If preferred, put the biscuits in a large plastic bag and bang and roll them with a rolling pin until they are crumbed finely.)
- Chop each 'Eskimo' into 8 slices, or each 'fruit puff' into 3 to 4 pieces, and mix them with everything else in the bowl.
- Form the mixture into 3 or 4 cylinders, roll these in coconut, then roll them in cling film and refrigerate for several hours or overnight. OR press the mixture into one end of a rectangular slice pan which has been lightly buttered or sprayed, then coated with coconut. Press the mixture out so it is about 2cm deep.
- Cut the cylinders into slices 10–15 mm thick just before serving, or cut the mixture in the slice pan into about 24 squares. (Do not put extra coconut over the cut surfaces or you spoil their bright appearance.)

Ginger Crunch

Ginger Crunch is another perennial New Zealand favourite. Even though it seems to have been around 'forever', it is still popular, and why not? It's delicious packed in a school lunch or enjoyed with a cup of tea or coffee.

For an 18 x 28cm slice

Base
125g butter
¼ cup sugar
1 tsp baking powder
1 cup standard flour
1 tsp ground ginger

Icing
2 Tbsp butter
2 tsp ground ginger
2 rounded Tbsp golden syrup
1 Tbsp water
2 cups icing sugar

- Heat oven to 180°C (or 170°C fan bake) with the rack just below the middle. Line the sides and bottom of a pan about 18 x 28cm with baking paper, allowing enough extra paper on the sides for lifting the cooked slice, or spray a 23cm square loose-bottomed pan.
- For base: Cut the cold butter into nine cubes, then process in brief bursts with remaining base ingredients, until the mixture is the texture of coarse breadcrumbs. If mixing by hand, warm butter until soft, mix it with the sugar, and then stir in the sieved dry ingredients.
- Spread the crumbly mixture into the pan and press it down firmly and evenly. Bake for about 10 minutes or until lightly browned. It will still feel soft while it is hot. While the base cooks, make the icing, as the base should be iced while hot.
- **For the icing:** Measure the butter, ginger, golden syrup and water into a small pot or microwave bowl. Heat, without boiling, until melted. Remove from the heat, sift in the icing sugar and beat until smooth. As soon as the base is cooked, pour over the warm icing and spread carefully so it covers the base evenly. Leave the square to cool and set, marking it into pieces while still warm. Do not remove from the pan until it has cooled completely. Store in an airtight container for up to a week.

NOTE: *If you like a really thick icing, use one and a half times the icing recipe quantities.*

Extra-easy Carrot Cake

We both thought 'good old' carrot cake would appear as being popular and are delighted that it did. This delicious version is so easy it seems almost too easy to believe. If you microwave it, you can be finished in less than 15 minutes!

For a 20cm ring cake
½ cup canola oil
1 cup brown sugar
½ cup milk
2 eggs
1 cup self-raising flour
1 tsp baking soda
½ tsp salt
½ cup chopped walnuts
1 tsp vanilla essence
2 tsp cinnamon
1 tsp mixed spice
¼–½ tsp grated nutmeg
200g grated carrot (2 medium)

- Heat the oven to 180°C.
- Measure the oil, brown sugar and milk into a large bowl. Break in the eggs and stir to combine. Add the remaining ingredients and stir until just combined.
- Non-stick spray a 20–21cm ring tin (7–10-cup capacity), then pour in the cake mixture. Bake for about 25 minutes, or until a skewer inserted in the middle comes out clean. (Alternatively, put the mixture in a microwave tin, cover with a paper towel, and microwave on High (100%) power for 8 minutes or until cooked.)
- Leave the cake to cool in the pan for about 5 minutes, then turn out onto a rack and cool completely before icing.

Cream Cheese Icing

1 cup cream cheese (regular or reduced fat)
½ cup icing sugar
zest of 1 lemon or ½ orange
pumpkin seeds and chopped dried apricots to decorate

- Measure the cream cheese and icing sugar into a bowl, add the citrus zest and stir until just combined.
- Spread icing over the cooled cake, then garnish with the pumpkin seeds and chopped dried apricots.

Banana Cake

Banana cake must be familiar to everyone raised in New Zealand. It provides the perfect way to use up brown-flecked bananas which are on sale because they are too ripe.

For a 21cm ring cake or a large loaf
150g butter, melted
1–1¼ cups ripe, mashed banana (about 3 bananas, mashed)
½ cup white sugar
½ cup brown sugar
1 tsp vanilla essence
2 large eggs
½ cup milk
2 cups self-raising flour

- Heat oven to 180°C (170°C fan bake), with rack just below middle. Coat a 20–21cm (7-cup capacity) ring pan or large loaf pan evenly with non-stick spray.
- Melt the butter until liquid in a large bowl in a microwave oven, or in a large pot, preferably with rounded corners, then remove from heat. Mash the bananas with a fork, working from one end to the other, without leaving chunks. (Slightly overripe bananas give the cake best flavour.) Tip into the pot or bowl along with the sugars, vanilla and eggs. Beat with a fork, stirrer or whisk until the eggs are well blended. Stir in the milk, then add the flour. Beat until evenly mixed, then pour into prepared cake pan.
- Bake for 40–50 minutes until top is golden brown, the centre springs back when pressed, and a skewer poked into the middle comes out clean. (Don't worry if the top cracks slightly.) Leave in the tin for 5 minutes, then invert onto a cooling rack. Serve plain, dusted with icing sugar, or iced with chocolate icing, preferably within a few hours of baking. This is particularly nice for dessert, served warm or with ice cream and fresh fruit.

EXTRA-EASY CARROT CAKE

LEMONADE & CREAM SCONES (TOP)
PIKELETS (BOTTOM)

Lemonade & Cream Scones

This isn't the traditional version of scones, but it is so easy, good and reliable, we will probably never go back to Grandma's version!

For 8 large square scones

2 cups (260g) self-raising flour

¼ cup sugar

½ tsp salt

½ cup cream

½ cup plus 2 Tbsp lemonade

- Heat oven to 230°C.
- Measure the dry ingredients into a large bowl. (Remember to fork the flour until light before measuring it, then to spoon it into the measuring cup and level off the top without packing it down or banging it.) Toss dry ingredients together, add the cream and lemonade, and mix to make a soft dough.
- Scrape the sides of the bowl and sprinkle enough extra flour over the ball of soft dough to allow you to turn it out onto a floured board and handle without sticking.
- Knead dough lightly, half a dozen times, then pat or roll it out until it is about 2cm thick, and twice as long as it is wide.
- Cut in half lengthways, and in four crossways, using a floured knife.
- Arrange scones on a baking tray (close together if you like soft sides, or further apart for crusty sides). For a good colour, brush tops with a little milk or melted butter.
- Bake for 10–12 minutes, until tops and bottoms are lightly browned.
- Serve warm (or reheated) with butter and jam, or spread with jam and top with whipped cream. Fresh strawberries or raspberries make an excellent addition.

NOTE: *These scones stay fresh and soft for 48 hours — if they get the chance!*

Pikelets

Many, many Kiwis remember their mothers and grandmothers turning out plates of pikelets and they still remain a great, quick snack for unexpected company. Spread with butter and jam, top the butter with hundreds and thousands for small children, or 'dress them up' with whipped cream, jam and fresh berries. Yum!

For 12–16 pikelets, depending on size

1 rounded Tbsp golden syrup

25g butter

1 Tbsp sugar

½ cup milk

1 large egg

1 cup self-raising flour

- Heat a frypan. (Use a high heat setting if frypan is electric.)
- Dip an ordinary tablespoon in hot water and then use it to measure the syrup. Put the syrup in a bowl with the butter. Warm (microwaving is easiest) to soften both, then mix in the sugar, milk and egg. Sprinkle or sieve the flour over the top, then mix it in briefly with a whisk or beater just until smooth.
- Rub surface of the hot frypan with a little butter on a paper towel. Drop dessertspoon or tablespoon portions of mixture into the pan, pouring mixture off the tip of the spoon. If you can manage to hold the spoon handle upright and turn the spoon as you let the batter run off it, you should get perfectly round pikelets.
- Turn pikelets over as soon as the bubbles begin to burst on the surface. (Turn up the heat if the cooked side of each pikelet is not brown enough OR turn heat down if they have browned too much by the time the first bubbles burst.) When the centres of the second side spring back when touched with your finger, the pikelets are ready. (If pikelets are too thick and are not spreading enough, add a little extra milk to mixture.)
- Cook in batches until all the batter is used. Keep cooked pikelets warm by putting them between the folds of a clean tea towel, and transfer them to a plastic bag when cold. Serve soon after making.

Anzac Biscuits

Anzac Biscuits taste good, last well if stored in airtight containers, and are easy to make! Let your children help and, if you have been a good teacher, it won't take long until they can make them all by themselves. Our family has made this version for years.

For about 50 biscuits

100g butter

¼ cup golden syrup

1 tsp vanilla

1 cup sugar

1 cup fairly fine rolled oats

1 cup desiccated coconut

1 cup plain flour

½ tsp baking soda

2 Tbsp warm water

- Heat the oven to 170°C (160°C fan bake) with a rack in the middle of the oven. Line a baking tray with baking paper or a Teflon liner.
- Melt the butter in a fairly large saucepan until it is liquid. Use levelled measuring cups and spoons to measure everything else. Add the golden syrup, take the pot off the heat and stir until butter and syrup are blended. Stir in the next five ingredients to the saucepan. Mix the baking soda and water. Add to the mixture in the pot and stir well. If the mixture seems too crumbly to mix easily, add 1–2 Tbsp of extra water, until it can be rolled into balls the size of cherry tomatoes. Put the balls on the baking paper leaving plenty of room for spreading. While they bake, shape more balls to go on the tray when the first lot are cooked.
- Bake for about 15 minutes, until the biscuits are evenly golden brown. Lift the warm biscuits onto a cooling rack. When cold, store in an airtight container.

VARIATIONS: *Add a cup of chopped roasted peanuts or chopped walnuts to the mixture before adding the sugar. Replace the coconut with an extra cup of rolled oats.*

Quick Chocolate Brownies

Brownies are very versatile — they make a great snack with tea or coffee and, served with vanilla ice cream, are a delicious dessert. This version is butter free, and for extra speed and convenience is microwaved. Microwaved brownies are soft-textured when served the day they are made, but do tend to become a bit firmer on standing. They are good both ways, just different!

For 6 large or 12 regular brownies

½ cup canola or other light
    vegetable oil

2 large eggs

1 cup sugar

1 tsp vanilla

½ tsp salt

½ cup self-raising flour

½ cup plain flour

¼ cup cocoa

¼–½ cup chopped walnuts (optional)

- Measure the oil, eggs, sugar, vanilla and salt into a medium-sized bowl and beat well with a fork.
- Measure the salt, flours and cocoa into a sieve over the bowl. Sift into the mixture and fold everything together evenly, using a stirrer or rubber scraper. Stir in the nuts if using.
- Line a 20cm square or 21 x 15cm rectangular microwave container with straight sides at least 6cm high, with a piece of cling film. Tip in the prepared mixture and spread evenly. Cover with a non-stick liner or baking paper. (Covering is important for even rising and cooking.)
- Stand the dish on an inverted plate so it is at least 1cm above the cooking surface. Microwave on High for 4–7 minutes, checking every minute after 4 minutes. Do not worry if the surface looks rather uneven, but don't take the brownies out of the microwave until they are dry on top. Cool in cooking container, then turn out onto a cutting board. When cold, cut into bars or other shapes.
- Dust the top with icing sugar, or turn the cut pieces in sifted icing sugar so all surfaces are covered. Serve with vanilla ice cream.

NOTE: *If preferred, bake brownies in a 20cm square baking paper-lined pan, at 180°C for 20–30 minutes or until a toothpick comes out clean.*

ANZAC BISCUITS

BLUEBERRY & ORANGE MUFFINS

Blueberry & Orange Muffins

From a historical perspective, muffins seem to have come from nowhere to claim a definite and well-deserved place in our national baking repertoire! Everybody seems to love them, and blueberry muffins remain the archetype. The addition of a little orange zest and juice freshens them up and brings out the flavour of the berries, but can be omitted if you want. We like the crunchy cinnamon sugar topping, but it's not essential.

For 12 regular-size muffins
2 cups standard flour
4 tsp baking powder
½ tsp salt
½ cup sugar
zest of ½ orange
100g butter
½ cup plain or fruit-flavoured yoghurt
½ cup orange juice
1 large egg
1–1½ cups blueberries (see note)
½ tsp cinnamon, optional
1 Tbsp sugar, optional

- Heat oven to 220°C (or 210°C fan bake) with the rack just below the middle.
- Sieve the first 4 ingredients into a fairly large bowl, and add the orange zest.
- In another container warm butter until melted, then add the yoghurt, orange juice and egg, and beat to mix thoroughly.
- Prepare fresh or partly frozen berries, then tip the liquid and fruit into the bowl with the dry mixture. Without overmixing, fold everything together. Flour should be dampened, not smooth. Berries should keep their shape.
- Divide the mixture evenly between 12 regular muffin pans that have been well coated with non-stick spray. Combine the remaining cinnamon and sugar and sprinkle this over the tops if desired.
- Bake for 12–15 minutes, until muffins spring back when pressed. (Muffins made with frozen berries will take about 5 minutes longer.)

NOTE: *Use frozen free-flow blueberries when fresh ones are not available. To stop frozen blueberries staining the batter, use them before they thaw completely.*

. . . .

Custard Kisses (Melting Moments)

Custard Kisses are certainly a favourite in our family — it's nice to know they're so popular with others too. There isn't anyone in our family (the full three generations) who can walk past a jar full of these without stopping for a little sample!

For about 20 filled kisses or 40 halves
175g butter, softened
1 cup icing sugar
1 tsp vanilla essence
1½ cups standard (plain) flour
½ cup custard powder
1 tsp baking powder

Vanilla Filling
50g butter, softened
1 cup icing sugar
2 Tbsp custard powder
a few drops of vanilla essence

- Heat oven to 180°C (170°C fan bake), with oven rack just below middle. Line a baking tray with baking paper or a Teflon liner.
- Warm butter until very soft but not melted. Mix in a large bowl (or process) with the icing sugar and vanilla until creamy, then sift in the flour, custard powder and baking powder. Mix well, squeezing bowl-mixed dough together by hand and adding a little milk if necessary.
- Roll mixture into about 40 small balls. Flatten each with your hand before putting on the prepared baking tray. Make a pattern on them with a dampened fork, the bottom of a patterned glass, or your fingers.
- Alternatively, form mixture into a cylinder and refrigerate or freeze until dough can be sliced without flattening. Cut into about 40 slices, then put on a baking tray, decorate as above, or leave plain.
- Bake for about 12 minutes, until biscuits feel firm, but have not browned. (Browned biscuits taste of burnt butter.) Cool on a rack, then sort into pairs of similar size. Stick together with Vanilla Filling or raspberry jam. Store in airtight containers when icing has set. Freeze for longer storage.
- For filling: Mix softened (but not melted) butter with the other icing ingredients until smooth, adding a few drops of water if necessary. Put filling in a small (but tough) plastic bag, cut off the corner and squeeze a blob of icing onto one biscuit of each pair. Do not press halves together until you have used up all the filling evenly.

VARIATION: *If you must, replace custard powder with cornflour!*

Index